BIG BOOK OF
TRUCKS

Steve Lanham

BIG BOOK OF
TRUCKS

First published in the UK in 2013

© Demand Media Limited 2013

www.demand-media.co.uk

Printed and bound in China

ISBN 978-1-909217-50-8

Contents

4 – 7   Introduction

8 – 15   The Origins of the Species

16 – 27   The Steam Wagon

28 – 35   World War I and the First American Invasion

36 – 45   After the Storm

46 – 55   How Many Wagon Wheels Does It Take

56 – 67   After the Crash

68 – 77   World War II

78 – 93   The Heyday of the British-built Truck

94 – 101   The Swinging Sixties

102 – 113   The Final Years

114 – 117   Diesel and ICE

118 - 125   From Functionality to Style – the Evolution of the Cab

Introduction

BELOW A 1924
Leyland Type A
3-ton flatbed truck
at the 1997 HCVS
Bournemouth to
Bath Run

For the best part of a hundred years, road lorries and delivery vans have formed an intrinsic part of Britain's transport infrastructure, supporting all manner of industries across the nation. Initially, the truck was used to convey goods and materials from a central point such as a railway station, dockside or harbour, and deliver them to the surrounding districts but as roads improved and motorways were built, larger and more powerful trucks were able to cover greater distances. As the government's axe fell on what they considered to be the lesser profit-making railway lines, demand for carrying freight by road increased.

During the first half of the 19th Century, a railway wagon was often referred to as a 'lurry' – an old English verb rarely seen in literature today, and meaning 'to pull' or 'tug'. When, in the 1870s a number of engineering firms

experimented with purpose-built commercial vehicles, 'lurry' seemed appropriate terminology. It was not until the years just prior to World War I, however, that the derivation 'lorry' was in regular use. In British motoring circles, the terms 'waggon' (later wagon), 'heavy goods vehicle' (HGV), 'large goods vehicle' (LGV) and 'juggernaut' (for articulated vehicles) have also found their way into the English language. On this side of the Atlantic, 'truck' is a relatively modern-day term to describe the largest categories of commercial vehicle whereas ever since

motorised vehicles began appearing on the dusty roads of North America, it has been used to refer to any load carrier larger than a family car. The word 'truck' is thought to have originated from $\tau\rho o\chi\acute{o}\varsigma$ (trokhos), the Greek word for wheel, and has also been used in the past to describe railway wagons as well as other small wheel-mounted carriages.

There is a huge variety of lorries and trucks on the road today, all plying the highways and byways of Britain, and each built to perform a specific role day in, day out, all year round.

ABOVE This beautifully restored 1950 Austin K4 was part of the National Benzole fleet until 1957

There are curtain-sided lorries and articulated trucks delivering pallets of essential items to supermarkets, local shops and businesses. Tankers convey flammable liquids such as petrol, ethanol and diesel, as well as combustible gases and less dangerous products such as milk and flour. Luton-style removals vans help to transfer furniture and personal belongings from one house to another. Concrete mixers blend cement with sand or gravel to provide construction sites with a ready-to-use supply of mortar, while dump trucks bring hard core stone to wherever roads are being laid or resurfaced. Low-loaders transport heavy track-laying machinery too

slow and cumbersome to be driven on the road and recovery trucks come to the rescue of stranded vehicles that have broken down. And when all the food has been consumed, the new washing machine's installed, the flat-packed wardrobe looks something like it does in the picture, when all the cardboard boxes, protective polystyrene, plastic bags and surplus packaging has been discarded, that unsung hero the refuse lorry will cruise the streets in search of dustbins, collecting rubbish, garden waste and recyclable products, and generally keeping Britain tidy.

Today, there is a constant flow of trucks undertaking long distance haul-

BELOW Pictured in 2008, this Foden was still being operated by Dovey Haulage of Southampton

BELOW RIGHT This 1932 Bedford WS Fish and Chip van was fitted with a Mabbott coal stove to heat the fat fryer

age over the length and breadth of Britain, Europe and further afield. Motorways allow the sort of freight once carried by rail to be moved from place to place with speed and for the country's economy, they are a lifeline. Among the modern day truck operators there have been huge logistics firms; James Irlam, Ken Thomas and of course 'Steady' Eddie Stobart to name but a few, providing a daily transport service to hundreds of manufacturers, supermarkets and other retail outlets. Until recently, James Irlam's fleet of trucks, for example, consisted of 350 tractor units and 700 trailers while the vehicles flying the actual Eddie Stobart flag numbered in excess of 2,250. In 2008, James Irlam was bought out by the Stobart Group to create one huge conglomerate with directors of the former company joining the Stobart board. With road congestion at an all time high, the Stobart Group has in the last few years chosen to revert back to rail transport as a means of moving bulk goods around the country. Only time will tell if this has a lasting effect on the future of the inter-continental road haulier.

In putting this book together, I would like to express my sincere appreciation to the following people for their invaluable help with historical research and use of images: Mike Bennett, Lee Foster, Alan Thompson, Fred Wood, Patrick Collins of the Reference Library and Jon Day of the Motoring Picture Library at the National Motor Museum, Beaulieu, and last but by no means least my dad, Mike Lanham, whose enthusiasm for all things transport-orientated and willingness to help out in any way he can, has always been invaluable with the research projects I have undertaken. Thank you one and all!

Steve Lanham
2012

ABOVE The author's painting of a newly out-shopped Foden steam wagon on a test run through Sandbach, Cheshire

Chapter 1

The Origins of the Species

BELOW Before the invention of motorised transport, all bulk goods were carried long distance by horse-drawn waggon

For thousands of years, traders have used wheeled transport to carry goods around the country. Before the invention of the self-propelled vehicle in the latter half of the 1700s, horse and ox were an essential form of motive power and with Britain remaining under Roman occupation between 43AD and 410AD, new straight roads were built and existing routes greatly improved so that food products, grain, minerals, stone, timber and armaments could be moved with relative ease over great distances. Teams of horses or ox were required to shift the heaviest loads and such practice proved costly, was extremely time consuming and often needed considerable planning especially when it came to feeding and watering the animals. Over the centuries there have been many ideas as to how this work could be undertaken without the use of animals for haulage.

It was not until 1770 that an inventor called Nicolas-Joseph Cugnot successfully demonstrated a full-size working steam carriage and the Fardier à Vapeur is generally recognised as the world's first self-propelled road vehicle. It was designed to carry armaments and artillery for Napoleon's army but in practice was ab ill-conceived three-wheeled contraption with a heavy boiler suspended ahead of the front steerable wheel. In this configuration, it proved rather unstable and eventually crashed through a wall, nearly destroying itself and the hapless Cugnot with it! Not surprisingly, only one was ever built and it would be more than thirty years before there appeared the next major milestone in self-propelled vehicle development.

ABOVE The 1769 Fardier à Vapeur built by Nicolas-Joseph Cugnot (Image: National Motor Museum/MPL)

On Christmas Eve, 1801, Andrew Vivian made a successful accent of the particularly demanding Camborne Hill in Cornwall aboard Richard Trevithick's unwieldy steam carriage. It created enormous interest and sparked the imagination of many an inventor. Patented a year later, The London Steam Carriage was marketed to carry a maximum of ten passengers, but unfortunately there were few businessmen interested enough to invest and the project was eventually abandoned.

The 19th Century saw Britain fully embrace engineering technology and by the end of the 1800s, she led the world in industrial development. A number of firms that would eventually become well-known for their manufacture of heavy goods vehicles were started at this time.

In a factory adjacent to Oxford Street, London, Maudslay Sons & Fields initially set out to build marine-type steam engines, whilst across the city in Fashion Street, Spitalfields, George Scammell was making a name for himself, first as a wheelwright, and later as a carriage maker when his business became G. Scammell & Nephew. In the county of Cheshire, Plant & Hancock were fabricating implements to speed up agricultural processes and one of their youthful employees was Edwin Foden. After serving his apprenticeship with the London & North Western Railway, Foden returned to the business, subsequently being made a partner.

On George Hancock's retirement in 1887, Edwin took over the reigns. Across

BELOW A replica of Richard Trevithick's London Steam Carriage at the 1996 Great Dorset Steam Fair

ABOVE A fully laden
Hallford petrol truck
of 1906

the country in Suffolk, similar equipment was leaving the Leiston factory of Richard Garrett & Sons whilst John Fowler & Company of Leeds were becoming renowned for their steam-driven ploughing engines. Down in the south, the Liquid Fuel Engineering Co. Ltd of East Cowes on the Isle of Wight had embarked on steam passenger vehicle and goods van production and W.A. Stevens was perfecting electrical technology at his Maidstone premises a decade before joining forces with Thomas Tilling.

In the mid-1880s and decades before turning their attention to bus and lorry manufacture, the Bristol Wagon and Carriage Works Ltd, an iron foundry specialising in rolling stock for railways, was commissioned to build a four-wheel horse-drawn vehicle of a size and type usually employed by travelling preachers and religious organisations. As the first vehicle designed specifically for touring holidays by road The Wanderer sparked a worldwide craze that eventually led to a huge multi-national leisure caravan industry. Meanwhile, Dartford-based engineering firm, J.&.E. Hall were attempting to perfect refrigeration units for ocean-going cargo ships. Hall's founder, Everard Hesketh, had specifically chosen to specialise in this sphere of technology having seen similar appliances demonstrated at the 1878 Paris Exhibition. One of the company's engineers, Alexander Marcet, was an early 'autocarist' in the local area and, ever keen to embrace new and exciting ideas, Hesketh decided

BELOW The revolutionary Dennis overhead worm-drive transmission concept that was used on commercial vehicles for nearly thirty years

in 1906 to branch out into the motor industry. But instead of producing private passenger vehicles, he recognised the business opportunities of building commercials. Acquiring a licence to assemble petrol-engine 3-ton trucks of the design patented by established Swiss firm Adoph Saurer, a new subsidiary called Hallford commenced production a year later.

In the last decade of the 1800s, it was cycling that encouraged a number of entrepreneurs to open workshops and begin trading. Such eminent names as Morris and Dennis started out as makers of pedal cycles before they were seduced into the world of automobile and heavy goods vehicle manufacture. John Dennis and his brother Raymond built De-Dion Bouton and Aster-engine tricycles and light cars for five years before creating their first experimental commercial chassis in 1904. This vehicle shared mechanical parts with

their 16/20hp 4-cylinder car as well as a revolutionary overhead worm-drive transmission – the first in Britain. The idea was not patented until 1914 but featured on all cars produced until 1915 and on all trucks until the early 1930s. In 1908, Dennis Brothers had launched the first in a long line of fire engines – a specialist type of vehicle with which they would later become renowned for the manufacture of. By 1914, Dennis were employing nearly 700 staff.

BELOW A 1916 Dennis N fire appliance which was operated by London Fire Brigade until 1933

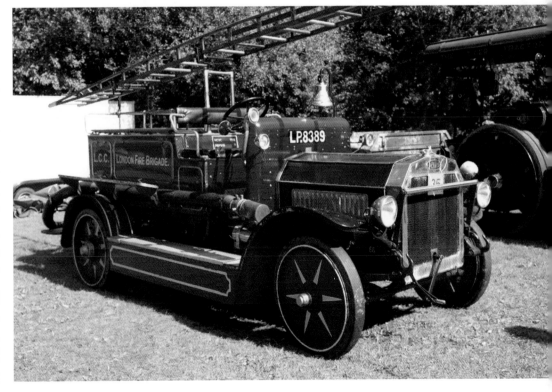

As the 19th Century came to a close, other names began to appear that would become inextricably intertwined throughout the history of motoring. Having gained the necessary experience from their previous employers, Mo-Car Syndicate Ltd, Thomas Blackwood Murray and Norman Osborne Fulton went into partnership with John

Henderson and began trading from their first-floor factory in Finnieston Street, Glasgow as the Albion Motor Car Company Ltd. Their first tentative steps into automobile production was a primitive dogcart featuring a flat-twin 8hp petrol engine. Over the next few years, however, their vehicles started to earn a reputation for

BELOW 1913 Albion A12 flatbed with 3,499cc petrol engine and prop-shaft drive

quality engineering and included a half-ton van in 1902. Nevertheless, it would be nearly ten years before the firm made any real commitment to creating commercial vehicles and by then the factories of Albion, New Arrol-Johnston Car Company Ltd (formerly Mo-Car), and Halley Industrial Motors Ltd would all be working to capacity making Glasgow the centre of Scottish lorry production.

With early motor manufacturers tapping into as many markets as possible, lightweight vans often represented nothing more than simple utility bodies fitted to existing automobile chassis and both private passenger cars and vehicles intended for traders and small businesses would often share the same assembly line. By the time Albion truck production was in full swing north of the border, to the south the Lacre Motor Car Company Ltd of Long Acre (hence the name) were receiving promising orders for their own trucks. To increase profits, they had applied to Albion to become the Scottish firm's London agent. As a sideline they had also started

publicising themselves as purveyors of motoring clothing and accessories, and coachbuilders for Wolseley and Lanchester. From 1910, Lacre were providing a range of commercial vehicles capable of carrying between 10cwt and 10-ton payloads – the flagship 38hp model being priced at £750.

With the factory at saturation, all proceedings were moved to Letchworth Garden City in Hertfordshire. With the goods vehicle market ever expanding, Lacre found that they were now competing with the likes of the Maudslay Motor Company of Coventry, Luton's Commercial Cars Ltd, the Southport-based Vulcan Motor & Engineering Co. Ltd, and in Wigan, Pagefield Commercial Vehicles, all vying for business in the highly popular light to medium weight truck sector.

ABOVE 1912 Lacre 2-ton box van

Chapter 2

The Steam Wagon

The world of trucks is today dominated almost exclusively by diesel powered giants thundering along our motorways the length and breadth of Britain, but it is important to recognise that in those embryonic years during Queen Victoria's reign, diesel power was not a viable option. Long before petrol engines made their high street debut aboard fragile 'horseless carriages', and certainly decades before a powerful and reliable diesel engine had been perfected, self-propelled transport relied on a number of largely unproven or at best rudimentary power sources. Steam engines, however, were beginning to demonstrate their worth in factories, mills and on the farm, and it was a challenge for many engineers of the time to adapt that knowledge for road transport purposes. Early wagons or, rather, experimental 'lurries' were built to perform particular tasks and John Yule, for example, constructed a one-off vehicle specifically designed for manoeuvring large marine boilers.

During the Industrial Revolution, when there were huge and exciting advances in factory production processes, engineering firms specialising in the manufacture of steam engines could equally turn their expertise and inventiveness to the development of road, rail and shipping technology. One such company was established by John Thornycroft on the banks of the River Thames to build water-borne craft. The race to create a dependable commercial carrier to replace horse-drawn vehicles had caught Thornycroft's imagination. At the time, the problem of London's overcrowded streets was compounded by the number carts, waggons and caravans belonging to itinerant vendors,

religious groups and showmen, and every taxi cab and two-wheeled trap relying, quite literally, on horse-power. In 1896, Thornycroft and his colleague, Colonel Niblett constructed a half-ton four wheel 'van' with a vertical boiler, chain-driven front wheels and tiller steering to the rear.

It was initially intended for passenger carriage but, its potential as transport for bulk goods and commodities was soon clear.

Another van of similar design was constructed later that same year by the recently founded Lancashire Steam Motor Company. This firm was set up by the son of a blacksmith in the little known village of Leyland. In time the village would lend its name the most influential organisation in the history of the British truck industry. When it came to building a steam wagon, there were two schools of thought as to the best location for the engine. Many firms embarking on steam wagon construction had formed their own ideas from years of manufacturing stationary, portable and traction engines. Influenced by the general layout of a traction engine, they often chose the 'overtype' where the cylinder block, cranks, and all the motion was placed on top of the boiler which in turn was mounted above the chassis. This meant, however, that much of the vehicle's superstructure was taken up by the actual steam engine leaving relatively less space for load carrying.

In 1897, Mann & Charlesworth of Leeds started building an overtype 'Steam Cart' that took the form of a design patented by P.J. Parmiter. Designed so that it could be driven by one person, the Steam Cart featured a completely detachable tipper-style bucket over the rear wheels making it particularly useful in industry and on the farm.

LEFT An omnibus built in 1900 by the Lancashire Steam Motor Company of Leyland

BELOW The Mann Patent Steam Cart

Although the vehicle generated much interest and orders were promising, in only a year the company was considering an 'undertype' wagon, so-called as the cylinders, cranks and motion were under-slung beneath the chassis. In this form, the driver's cab took up less room affording greater capacity for cargo. The downside was that due to the rough conditions of unpaved roads and tracks across the country, the essential work-

BELOW 1901 Thornycroft 5nhp 5-ton wagon, Works No.39 at the 1994 Great Dorset Steam Fair

ings exposed and in such close proximity to the ground were forever prone to damage. Sales of the overtype, however, prompted Mann to concentrate on Steam Cart manufacture and such was its success that by 1900, the company had changed its name to Mann's Patent Steam Cart & Wagon Co. Ltd.

John I. Thornycroft & Co., Ltd had also turned their attention to the overtype and moved all factory proceedings to larger premises in Basingstoke, Hampshire to begin mass production.

1896 and 1903 were turning points in the fortunes of the early steam wagon and production stepped up a pace following the passing in Parliament of the Light Locomotive Acts. New legislation meant that a heavy goods vehicle or traction engine weighing five tons or less did not legally require a crew of three (consisting of driver, steersman and a red flag man walking in front) and could now be designed for just single-person operation. The amended rules

ABOVE This 1912 Wallis & Steevens spent its early working life under the ownership of J.W. Lance of Lymington, Hampshire

benefited a number of small (albeit mostly short-lived) back-street firms who could get a better foothold in the commercial vehicle market. The choice of steam wagon for businesses relying on the collection and delivery of goods rapidly became wide and varied with such names as Bretherton & Bryan, English, Gillett, Hercules, Pioneer and Simpson-Bibby entering the scene.

One of the strangest vehicles to emerge from this period was the 'Manchester'. Any tradesman who already owned a horse-drawn dray could replace the horse element by attaching to the front pivot point the 'Manchester', a two wheel fore-carriage containing a vertical boiler and powered by an engine made by Turner, Atherton & Co., Ltd, Denton. For the time being, the overtype remained the most popular configuration amongst manufacturers such as the Cheshire firm, E. Foden, Sons & Company, W. Taskers & Sons of Andover, and their Hampshire neighbours Wallis & Steevens Ltd – like Thornycroft another firm hailing from Basingstoke.

B. O'GORMAN & SONS
Steam Haulage
NEWBRIDGE

M 8681

Foden had marginally lost out to Thornycroft at the 1901 War Office Trials at Aldershot. On paper, the Foden entry with its unorthodox outside-frame rear axle looked the clear winner ahead of its closest rival. When the result was upheld, however, the dispute became the subject of a lively debate in Parliament. The free publicity that this alone gave Foden was enough impetus to start serious production.

Even though most engineering works were opting for the overtype, the undertype was still being championed by a few devotees. The Yorkshire Patent Steam Wagon Company stayed loyal to the overtype right up until 1937 when the last steam lorry left their Leeds works. Their distinctive transverse double-ended boiler design had a split smokebox and central header chamber funnelling exhaust gases through the chimney, Another undertype proponent

was the Glasgow engineering firm of Alley & McLellan. Established in 1906, they extensively developed their range of 'Sentinel' wagons and eventually gained a reputation as the world's leading undertype maker. When, in 1915, expansion warranted a relocation to Shrewsbury in Shropshire, 'Sentinel' was so well-known that it was adopted as the company name.

LEFT Foden 4nhp 5-ton wagon No.6350 at the 2006 Great Dorset Steam Fair

BELOW 1914 Yorkshire WE 3-speed 6-ton wagon

A steam wagon was not without its merits and on a good day, a Foden for example could travel 30 miles on one tank of water and had enough coal capacity for 40 miles. They were particularly effective forms of transport during World I when all factory output was geared towards building wagons destined to be munitions and supply carriers in support of troops on the ground. Unfortunately, the war was partly to blame for the demise of the steam wagon. With British manufacturing stretched to the limit, the

Government called on their allies across the Atlantic to supply additional equipment. The United States was happy to oblige and throughout the conflicts a steady stream of heavy machinery was imported to speed up essential farming and timber processes. Thousands of American-built motor lorries eased the strain on battle-weary vehicles at the front line and when the Armistice was declared in 1918, the Ministry of Defence was left with huge stocks of perfectly useable trucks. With hostilities at an end, the decision was made to sell off surplus equipment and suddenly the market was flooded with cheap petrol-engine commercial chassis. It was far easier, more cost effective and indeed cleaner for an owner of a petrol or diesel-powered lorry to throw the engine into life via the starting handle than to light and maintain a fire, and wait for the boiler to heat up enough to raise sufficient steam pressure. Added to that, all the essential workings and fuel tank of a petrol lorry were neatly

BELOW Atkinson 6-ton wagon No.72

ABOVE Fowler
No.19708 Pendle Prince
built in 1931

stowed under a bonnet or beneath the cab floor affording greater payload space.

By the mid-1930s, nearly all companies that had in time become world-renowned for their steam-driven commercials had either conceded to internal-combustion engine vehicle production or, like so many before, ceased trading. The powers that be at Foden's Elworth Works in Sandbach were particularly slow and reluctant to embrace modern thinking. In a last ditch attempt to turn the tide they started building undertypes, but the writing was on the wall.

If it had not been for Edwin Foden retiring from the Board and subsequently helping son, Dennis, set up his own business under the banner ERF, Foden may never have capitulated to launch their series of diesel lorries in 1932. Foden steam wagon production lasted only two more years.

Struggling to compete with their

adversaries, it was also time for Atkinson of Preston to call a halt on their sixteen years of creating steam vehicles and under new ownership, begin an era rejuvenated under the name Atkinson Lorries (1933) Ltd. It was a very different story for other less fortunate firms who disappeared from the truck manufacturing scene altogether. John Fowler & Co. closed in 1935 whilst an earlier casualty was Richard Garrett & Sons Ltd, bringing to an end 28 years of steam wagon production having completed their first in 1904.

The only firm to buck the trend was Sentinel who continued to concentrate on technical developments, periodically unveiling updated driving cabs, refining boiler and motion engineering, and improving transmission. In the last full decade of steam wagon production, they introduced the carden (propeller) drive shaft with a conventional lorry rear axle on the 'S' type and, in 1929, the Sentinel DG8 with dual front steering

– the first rigid eight-wheeler in Britain.

Capable of reaching speeds in excess of 60mph, the 'S' was the pinnacle of wagon design and could well have been a competent alternative to the motor lorry, but it was all a little too late. After World War II, Sentinel were the only steam wagon builders in Britain and steadfastly soldiered on until the late 1940s. Nearly all new orders were taken from investors in South America and some models were even built under licence – a range of 4, 5 and 6-tonners, for example, emerging from Skoda's Mlada Boleslav railway locomotive works in Czechoslovakia. With all but a tiny minority of hauliers operating petrol or diesel trucks, the last batch left the Shrewsbury factory in 1949 destined for Argentina and Sentinel finally closed the chapter on the British-built steam wagon for good.

ABOVE 1932 Sentinel DG4 No.8666 tar tanker on the 1997 HCVS London to Brighton Run

Chapter 3

World War I and the First American Invasion

In the first decade of the 20th Century, Britain was one of the most prosperous countries on Earth, leading the world in ship building, textiles and foreign investments. In the years prior to World War I, many names appeared that would influence development within the British truck industry over the following decades.

The ubiquitous Ford Model T had matured into the TT and the company's brand new Trafford Park facility in Manchester churned them out at a pace. Another company hailing from Manchester, this time from the eastern district of Clayton and whose reputation was built on good quality and reliable fire appliances, was Belsize Motors Ltd.

Their commercial vehicle department, however, was short-lived with only a comparatively small number of trucks destined for private ownership leaving the Clayton plant between 1911 and 1915.

In the meantime, Hallford – a name derived from the combination of J.&.E. Hall (ship refrigeration unit makers) and their home town of Dartford – had become well-established lorry manu-facturers. These had especially found favour as brewery drays but customers also included London County Council where numerous chassis were put to use sporting coachbuilt bus bodies. During the 1900s, Hallford had collaborated with electrical engineers W.A. Stevens of Maidstone to develop petrol-electric buses where the petrol engine generated enough electricity to power a motor driving the rear wheels.

ABOVE This 1915 Daimler CB22 3-ton truck was on display at the Dean Forest Railway in 1997

LEFT This 1912 Belsize pump escape, powered by an immense 14,680cc petrol engine was operated by Southampton City Fire Brigade

The idea had been the brainchild of inventor Percival Frost-Smith, and proved simpler to operate than a conventional petrol engine vehicle in a time when few driver's had experience of using a crash gearbox. The joint project only lasted a few years, however, and came to an end when Thomas Tilling invested his own money into W.A. Stevens and formed Tilling-Stevens Ltd to build a similar product under the new brand.

In the last two decades of the 1800s, Britain was embroiled in quelling civil unrest amongst Dutch settlers in the Transvaal region of Southern Africa. During the resulting Boer War mechanised transport proved its worth in moving artillery, ammunitions, supplies and troops. Traction engines had been especially useful hauling trains of armoured personnel wagons and the heaviest gun carriages, and with escalating unrest between certain states across Europe in the first few years of the 20th Century, the British Government decided that there was a growing need for a reserve pool of trucks in case of future conflicts. In 1911, a national subsidy scheme was introduced where relatively low-priced motor lorries could be bought individually or in fleets on condition that if any military campaign entailed extra transportation, owners were required to relinquish their vehicles up to 48 hours after notification.

A number of established truck manufacturers put forward suitable designs with the most versatile and adaptable gaining War

BELOW 1917 Leyland 34hp carrying a Southern Railway removals container

Office approval. Pagefield's offering was the 4-ton N-Type, a rugged workaday model that remained in their catalogue right up to 1931. N-Types fitted with tipper truck bodies featured the company's own patent tipping mechanism that utilised the gearbox to power a screw-driven lifting ram.

In Huddersfield, Karrier Motors Ltd were building the B4-Type. Formerly trading under the name, Clayton & Co., Karrier had earned a reputation for creating vehicles ideal for traversing rough ground and overcoming steep inclines. Soon the B4 would prove invaluable to the Allies in parts of war-torn France.

BELOW An immaculate Thornycroft flat-bed truck at the 2008 Basingstoke Transport Festival

ABOVE 1917 AEC
V Type at the 1994
HCVS Bournemouth to
Bath Run

Leyland, Thornycroft and Tilling-Stevens had all met with government endorsement and collectively, these companies provided thousands of chassis for military use, not only for the British armed forces, but many saw service under French, Belgian, Canadian, Indian and later American flags.

The Associated Equipment Company, more commonly known as AEC were established in 1912 when the Underground Electric Railway Company made its road chassis-building activities a separate concern. The UERC road vehicle department was a huge organisation in its own right resulting from the merger in 1908 of the London Motor Omnibus Co., and the London General Omnibus Co. Bus construction was AEC's main area of employment and had signed an agreement with Daimler who would market chassis not destined for use in the capital. But the war intervened. With all hands to the pump and AEC coming under state control for the duration,

As events in Austro-Hungary and the Balkan states unfolded, production of national subsidy vehicles was stepped up and only three years after the programme was introduced, operators who had bought into the scheme found themselves honouring their obligation and surrendering vehicles for frontline use. Trucks ranging from between half-ton and 5-tons tendered by Albion, Commercial Car Ltd, Dennis, Hallford,

essential truck manufacture only really commenced in 1916. Even so 10,000 of their Y-Types alone were sent across the English Channel to help the war effort. AEC's output was greatly enhanced with flow-line assembly, each vehicle slowly travelling whilst under construction the length of AEC's Walthamstow factory.

Not all manufacturers were able to continue vehicle mass-production as their engineering skills were desperately required for other important duties. The Maudslay Motor Company, for example, were commandeered into making aero engines for the Royal Flying Corps.

Guy Motors Ltd of Wolverhampton were also building aero engines as well as becomeing the Royal Navy's largest supplier of depth charge fuses. Palladium Autocars of Putney had only been in business a short while when they, along with Wolseley, were put in charge of assembling the nicely proportioned Sopwith TF2 Salamander – the RAF's ground attack biplane.

Halley were busy making artillery shells and Vulcan Motor Engineering concentrated on the supply of other munitions at their Southport prem-

ises. Vulcan, incidentally, would later become the first organisation in Britain to sponsor a football team after buying Southport Football Club in 1918.

It was clear from the first two years of fighting that demand for mechanised transport was somewhat outstripping supply and Britain asked their allies, the United States for help.

ABOVE This Foden was originally built as a haulage tractor before conversion to a five-ton tipper truck and shipped to France around 1917

Thousands of American-built trucks were shipped across the Atlantic not only to join their European counterparts amongst the mud and trenches of Flanders but also to address the sudden shortfall of civilian transport back in Blighty. In 1916, the Gramm-Truck Co., of Lima, Ohio began shipping knocked-down kits of their all-terrain 'power wagons' to the Moseley Motor Works, Birmingham where they were put back together again. Proprietor, Henry Garner, had commenced business in 1907 and by 1912 claimed to be "The Largest Austin Salesman in the Kingdom"! When peace was finally declared in 1918, Garner and his Moseley concern continued to build trucks under licence before designing his own in the mid-1920s.

British trucks of the war years benefited enormously when pneumatic tyres were introduced to replace solids. The Goodyear Tyre and Rubber Co., of Akron, Ohio, had opened their UK headquarters in 1913 and four years later were promoting heavy duty compounds especially for commercial vehicle use. Not to be outdone, their biggest rival, Dunlop, followed suit soon after.

Post-War military depots were overflowing with surplus American vehicles, most notably FWDs, in addition to those pressed into service through the national subsidy scheme. The FWD was developed as an all-wheel-drive, all-terrain vehicle and for the next few years after the war, it was not uncommon to see an example on the British high street, earning its keep

BELOW 1917 USA Liberty truck at the 1995 HCVS London to Brighton Run

in private hands. FWDs were especially popular with fairground and circus operators.

Times were changing and some firms who had successfully built their business reputation on civilian commercial vehicle production before the war now looked into new and relatively untapped markets. Lacre, for example, chose to specialise in road sweepers – not exactly glamorous it has to be said or was it

a new idea having first been patented in America at the start of the Century. For the Hertfordshire-based company, however, it would represent bread and butter income for the next thirty years. Indeed, two of their employees, J.S. Drewry and Harry Shelvoke would, in the early 1920s, break away and form their own brand S&D, again largely concentrating on road sweeper and refuse lorries.

ABOVE This Locomobile was typical of the type of lorry supplied by the United States during World War I, and coming under civilian ownership after the Armistice

Chapter 4

After the Storm

With war in Europe at an end, the people of Britain yearned for a return to normality. With almost a million citizens killed in the terrible carnage, every community across the country had been affected especially when entire brigades of young men wiped out in the fighting were often from the same villages and towns. But on the eve of a new decade, it looked as though the 1920s was going to be a time of economic prosperity. Telephones were making communication between businesses quicker and easier, and nearly all who had suffered the hardships during World War I were beginning to enjoy their leisure time. Dance halls allowed young adults to let off steam on a Saturday night, Radios were providing entertainment in the home and, at the cinema, colour movies were introduced in 1922 although it would be another five years before 'talkies' were all the rage.

After the ravages of trench warfare, returning servicemen were keen to get back in the swing of everyday life again and some of them were eager to use new skills learnt in the armed forces.

Electricity was being used to greater effect both domestically and in industry, and on vehicles, night driving was improved enormously when paraffin and acetylene were rapidly being phased out in favour of electricity for head, side and tail lamps.

For the last five years, AEC had predominantly concentrated on its Y-Type national subsidy truck for the War Office and instead of spending precious time, money and effort coming

ABOVE 1919 Leyland 34hp 4-ton van

up with something new, immediately set about marketing the Y-Type for civilian use. But without the imposed constraints essential during a time of conflict, thoughts would soon turn to a new range of vehicles and over the next decade, the AEC catalogue included 2½, 4 and 6 ton trucks.

Thornycroft, like AEC, decided not to waste time getting the production lines rolling again and launched the X-Type which was basically a civilian version of their own offering in the national subsidy scheme.

Up until 1919, Dennis Brothers had been relying on other manufacturers' engines to power their vehicles but in that year, they purchased their main provider, White and Poppe of Coventry, so that they now had a say in the design and development of power units to suit their needs, have a ready supply of engines in-house, and also profit from engine sales to other vehicle producers.

Meanwhile in America, Clessie Cummins had just commenced diesel engine production but it would be

BELOW Bristol 4-ton drop-side truck

another ten years before Cummins were supplying power units en mass to many of Britain's truck manufacturers.

After a brief period of prosperity, Britain's industry began to suffer from increasing foreign competition. Sales had gradually slowed and a number of lorry producers fell foul of a post-war slump in the commercial vehicle market. Over the next few years, Atkinson, Caledon, Commercial Cars Ltd, Hallford, Lacre and McCurd, all ran into difficulties, adding to the rising number of unemployed.

The McCurd Lorry Manufacturing Company had been started in 1912 by Wallace Atherton McCurd as a relatively minor enterprise. Operating out of Hayes in Middlesex, it ceased trading altogether in 1927 have stuttered through the early 1920s.

Production of the Dorman-engine Caledon 4-ton lorry was started in 1915 by the Scottish Commercial Cars Company, a former agent for the Luton-based Commercial Cars Ltd. The height of factory activity was during the war when 400 4-tonners were built for military duty. In peacetime, the company re-launched itself as Caledon Industrial Motor Vehicles and a promis-

ing development was their Buda-engine 10-ton six-wheeler of 1924. Two years later, a General Strike was called to support the miners in their bid to improve appalling terms of employment. Entries in Caledon's order book fell and the company was bought out by Garrett, desperate to introduce petrol-power in an attempt to bolster flagging steam wagon sales. The project failed and both Garrett and Caledon had disappeared from the scene by the early 1930s.

BELOW A 1924 Albion SB24 24hp van in the livery of McVitie & Price Digestive Biscuits

Hallford had already gone by 1925 and in 1928, Lacre was downsized leaving municipal road sweepers as their only major offering.

Atkinson were slightly more fortunate. Much of their business was in steam wagon repair, opening servicing centres in Frenchwood, Preston and Freemason's Row, Liverpool. Edward Atkinson appeared to be clutching at straws when he bought the production rights to steam wagon replacement parts from Leyland and Mann. With finances in disarray, Atkinson joined forces in 1929 with Walker Bros., mining engineers based in Wigan and makers of Pagefield lorries. As Atkinson-Walker Waggons, this conglomerate briefly struggled on but was almost immediately hit by the global repercussions felt from the Wall Street Crash. Walker and Atkinson parted company with the latter calling in the official receivers soon after. It was not until 1933 when

BELOW The ubiquitous Ford Model T, this time in brewers dray form, built in 1926

Atkinson came under the ownership of a London garage proprietor could the newly reformed Atkinson Lorries (1933) Ltd start to trade on an even keel once more and drop steam wagon production altogether in favour of a more contemporary diesel-powered design. It was not all doom and gloom, however, and even though Commercial Cars Ltd and Halley Industrial Motors ran into their own financial difficulties during the 1920s, they were both rescued at the eleventh hour.

In 1926, Humber of Coventry bought Commercial Cars Ltd lock, stock and barrel, renamed it Commer Cars and from then on concentrated any goods vehicle manufacture at Commer's Luton site.

After coming under the custodianship of the North British Railway Company in 1927, Halley was absorbed by fellow Glasgow neighbours Albion in 1935 simply to eradicate the competition! In the intervening years, Albion had gone from strength to strength,

ABOVE 1929 Commer Type 23GN

finally ending production of their War Office subsidy truck in favour of a more up-to-date range that featured forward control cabs and shaft drive to the rear axle. In 1923, they embarked on bus manufacture and, but for a gap during World War II, would form the factory's main occupation for the next sixty years.

AFTER THE STORM

The American involvement in World War I had highlighted the potential of lucrative earnings in Europe for Stateside truck manufacturers. During the 1920s, several companies were set up to either import or mass produce trucks of American design.

The first to appear was the result of a joint venture between Crossley Motors Ltd of Gorton in Manchester and the Willys-Overland Company of Toledo, Ohio. In 1920, truck parts were manufactured and brought over from Canada, then a Dominion of the British Empire, to minimise import duties. At Heaton Chapel in Stockport, an ex-Air Ministry aeroplane factory was purchased and assembly began with new vehicles being initially sold as Willys-Overland Crossleys. By 1926, their 25cwt truck was being advertised under the 'Manchester' brand and two years later, having dropped models of American outline in favour of home-grown creativity, they assumed the Willys-Manchester banner. Next were Dodge Brothers of Detroit, one of the best selling car marques in the United States who opened their London branch in 1922, specifically to market their light commercial vehicles. In 1925 Peerless

BELOW 1927 Vulcan 20hp drop-side truck at the 1995 HCVS London to Brighton Run

P. J. KILBY

RX 2663

ABOVE 1926 Austin Heavy 12/4, Southsea Rally, 2001

and Chevrolet joined the fray.

Slough Lorries and Components Ltd specialised in reconditioning military trucks focussing mainly on Peerless. When war ended, they were left with a large supply of surplus Peerless parts but retained good relations with the Ohio-based manufacturer.

They reformed as the Peerless Trading Company, imported new parts to supplement their own stock and began building complete trucks from the ground up. For several years, Vauxhall Motors Ltd assembled light trucks at their Hendon plant. Like the Willys-Overland Crossley, this was basi-cally a vehicle built from parts (this time by Chevrolet) shipped over from Canada. But by the mid-1920s, even this well-established motoring giant had felt the impact of the post-war depression and was only just keeping its head above water. General Motors saw Vauxhall's plight as an opportunity

BELOW 1929 Ford Model AA

to get a foothold in Europe. In taking control for the princely sum of $2.5 million when the exchange rate was $4.87 to the British pound, GM had secured a bargain. The Canadian-built trucks were already being marketed as 'British Chevrolet' and GM saw no reason to change this as it seemed to help with sales. Production, however, was moved to Luton and the first new model, the 30cwt U-Type powered by a 6-cylinder engine went on sale in 1929.

Among the British companies who had managed to weather the economic downturn and hold their own against the American post-war influx were Dennis, Karrier, Leyland, Maudslay, Morris, and Scammell and newcomer, Bean Cars Ltd, all patiently biding their time until the worst of the storm had passed and capitalising on any financial backing they could secure. Despite the global and national monetary issues, there was still a wide choice of commercial vehicles on offer ranging from light 1-ton vans, heavy trucks for 10-ton payloads and timber tractors. Air and hydraulic brakes were being fitted as standard and the pneumatic had all but rendered the solid tyre redundant. The 1920s was also a period when articu-

lated trucks were becoming increasingly prevalent and Guy, Scammell, Thornycroft and Vulcan were all jumping on the non-rigid bandwagon.

BELOW This Karrier WO6 fitted with a 36hp Dorman engine was designed and built in 1929 for War Office use

Chapter 5

How Many Wagon Wheels Does It Take…

BELOW 1898 Thornycroft articulated steam tractor and semi-trailer

At the end of the 1800s, vehicle axle weight had increased beyond the possible comprehension or foresight of civil engineers who built Britain's roads and bridge structures during the preceding century. With the coming of the traction engine, the downward forces exerted directly onto the road was enormous and incidents resulting from surface collapse was becoming problematic.

The Road Traffic Act of 1930 is famed for its introduction of the driver's licence and driving test. The Act also included legislation that gave local government greater authority in enforcing strict regulations on maximum gross weight limits. For the heavy traction engine operator, higher tariffs were imposed which meant that for this form of transport at least, its days were numbered. Other exceptionally large vehicles were naturally affected and lorry producers looked into ways of

further spreading the load born on each axle. In 1930, however, the articulated lorry was by no means a new idea.

As early as the late-1890s, vehicles intended for commercial use were being designed as haulage tractor units with matching 'semi-trailers' i.e. a non-powered rear-axle carrier requiring the towing vehicle (or, if not in use, a retractable 'dolly') to keep it on an even plain.

Certainly in the first few years of the 20th Century, John I. Thornycroft & Co., Ltd were progressing with their steam 'van' idea and, in 1898, built one of the world's first articulated trucks.

In 1909, the Knox Automobile Company of Springfield, Massachusetts

introduced a coupling device so that the semi-trailer could easily be detached from the tractor unit. It consisted of a king pin on the trailer and, on the tractor, a 'fifth wheel' a quick release clamp surrounded by a u-shaped location guide.

ABOVE 1926 Scammell S10 articulated lorry on display at the 2002 Great Dorset Steam Fair

LEFT An American Knox articulated brewers dray dating from 1910

BELOW Only two of Scammell's enormous '100 Tonner' tractor units were ever built and both date from 1927. This example is a participant on the annual HCVS London to Brighton Run during the 1970s

From then on, all Knox articulated trucks were sold fitted with their patent fifth wheel coupling.

London haulier, Edward Rudd, had purchased such a vehicle from Knox and, recognising its potential, persuaded his local truck manufacturer, G. Scammell & Nephew to build something similar. Company founder, George Scammell's great nephew, Lieutenant

Colonel Alfred George Scammell had served in the army during World War I and having seen articulated trucks in action on the front line, returned home in 1918 with useful ideas as to how the Knox design could be improved. Two years later Scammell unveiled their version at the London Motor Show and on the single-axle semi-trailer sides was proudly proclaimed that the 7½ ton maximum payload could be carried at the cost and speed of 3 tons. The resultant influx of orders turned the fortunes of the company who upped sticks from their Spitalfields factory and relocated to new works in Watford to cope with demand. Their trailer design was gradually developed and put to use in all manner of industries including timber and logging and at various quarries round the country as a stone carrier. Shell-Mex Ltd, for example, ran a fleet of tankers, initially of square construction before the round tank was perfected. In 1926, Scammell launched the world's first frameless tanker where the round container acted as a stressed member.

Amongst other companies to begin production of articulated tractor and trailer units during the 1920s were Guy

ABOVE Scammell
MH3 Mechanical Horse
beautifully restored in
Great Western Railway
colours

and Vulcan (both launching their offerings in 1922), and a few years later, AEC.

1929 saw Scammells largest ever model, the '100 Tonner' low loader put into operation. Publicised as the largest truck in the world, it was powered by the company's own 7,094cc petrol engine tuned from 80bhp to 86bhp and returning a fuel consumption of 0.75 miles per gallon! The semi-trailer came in two versions, both measuring 50 feet in length but one built to carry a 100-ton payload, the other to carry 65-tons. Fitted with rear wheel steering to overcome tights corners, communication between tractor driver and rear steersman was either via a telephone system or with the use of whistles! Only two complete outfits were ever built. The first was delivered to Marston Road Services and was regularly used to transport the largest steam railway locomotives from Kitson's Leeds railway works over the Pennines to Liverpool Docks for export abroad. The second vehicle went to H.E. Coley of Dartford. Having continued to perform sterling work during the early 1920s, both examples were operated under the banner of specialist heavy-haulage contractor, Norman E. Box before Pickford's took over.

They were finally retired from active service just prior to World War II and have both survived into preservation, one at the British Commercial Vehicle Museum, Leyland, the other having been last recorded at a used truck dealership in Hitchin, Hertfordshire.

In 1931, Karrier announced a range of vehicles that would save precious turn-around time when distributing goods from the railway depot, therefore speeding up deliveries. The 3-ton Cob

BELOW Scammell Scarab on show at Horsted Keynes Station on the Bluebell Railway, 2003

and its bigger brother, the 4-ton Cob Major, were diminutive three-wheeled trucks available as either articulated tractor units with matching semi-trailers or as small, neat and highly manoeuvrable rigid municipal vehicles. The semi-trailer was later made in 'road-rail' form featuring railway wheels on an extra axle allowing the vehicle to be moved by rail if required.

Scammell's reputation for rail-associated transport was inexplicably sealed in 1934 with introduction of the Mechanical Horse, a rival to the Cob. This was a project started as a sideline three years earlier by the celebrated car makers, D. Napier & Sons Ltd, Lambeth but abandoned when their bid to buy out Bentley was dastardly scuppered by Rolls-Royce. Thereafter Napier lost interest in the motor industry choosing instead to concentrate on aviation engines and sold all production rights of the Mechanical Horse to Scammell. The Mechanical

Horse could be ordered in 3 or 6-ton form powered by a 1,125cc or 2,043cc side-valve petrol engine respectively. Above the rear axle was fitted an automatic coupling mechanism allowing the driver to reverse up to and attach a semi-trailer without the inconvenience of leaving the cab. If one adds the fact that the front steerable wheel could rotate laterally allowing a turning circle less than the overall length of the entire articulated vehicle, it can be seen that the Mechanical Horse was an extremely useful device. All of the 'Big Four' railway companies, namely the GWR, LMS, LNER and Southern, as well as the Royal Mail placed orders with Scammell and up and down the country, it was a common sight to see one of these vehicles scampering to and from the local railway yard. On the Continent, Chenard et Walcker of Gennevilliers, France, built a version under licence and appropriately marketed it as the

Pony Mécanique.

The Mechanical Horse was superseded in 1948 by the Scammell Scarab which in turn was replaced by the Townsman. The last of these left the Watford assembly plant in 1968 bringing the total number produced since 1934 to 30,000 with over 100,000 matching trailers.

ABOVE A 1967 Scammell Townsman participating in the 2001 Bournemouth to Bath Run. Alongside is the Townsman's predecessor, the Scarab, in British Road Services Parcels livery

HOW MANY WAGON WHEELS DOES IT TAKE

BELOW A 1935 Leyland TSC8 Beaver (a typical 4x2 rigid), at the 1995 Nobles Park Rally, Isle of Man

Today's UK road legislation allows for a 'gvm' or gross vehicle mass (in other words the combined weight of truck and load) of 44,000kg. To lessen the downward forces on the road surface, there will normally be three axles on the tractor unit and three on the trailer, spread as far apart without compromising manoeuvrability.

As Department of Transport rules have changed to accommodate heavier vehicles, so have the rules relating to vehicle length. Although any vehicle carrying a load of an abnormally large size and length is allowed to use British roads, they are the subject of

certain restrictions if, in the case of an articulated lorry, measure longer than 75 feet. Moving such objects requires careful planning, consultation with the Department of Transport as to the best route to follow, and a designated escort vehicle provided by either the haulage company or in some cases, the police.

The alternative to the articulated lorry is the 'rigid' where two, three or four load-bearing axles share a common non-pivoting chassis. The maximum length permitted on British roads without an escort vehicle is 60 feet.

Generally speaking, there are four types of rigid: The '4x2' is probably the most widespread rigid seen on today's busy roads and simply denotes a four-wheeled lorry with final drive to the rear two wheels. To avoid confusion, even if the rear axle has twin-rear wheels on either side of the differential, in Britain it is still referred to as a four-wheeler.

A '6x4' is a six-wheeled vehicle with final 'double drive' to the two rear axles consisting of four wheels – two per axle. Again, the '6' ignores the fact that there may be twin sets of wheels per rear axle but, just to complicate matters, in some countries this type is called a ten-wheeler! 6x4s are ideal transport for

conveying heavy materials over rough and soft ground and make particularly effective tipper trucks.

ABOVE A 4x6 rigid in the form of a 1950 Foden FE6/12 (12-tonner)

BOWATERS

114   114

BYV 561

ABOVE This 8x4 rigid AEC Mammoth Major in Bowaters Paper Mills livery has twin-steering front axles

The term '6x4 Tag' refers to a six wheeled truck that has a front steerable axle, a central driving axle and a free-wheeling 'tag' axle at the rear that can be lifted off the road surface. This is done for two reasons; it reduces drag and fuel consumption when the vehicle is empty or, if required, can also help with grip by increasing weight distribution to the central driving axle.

A '6x4 Mid-Lift' is very similar to

the '6x4 Tag' except that the rear axle is driven and the central free-wheeling axle also known as a 'pusher' can be raised or lowered. The latter can also be fitted with steering, aiding manoeuvrability through tight corners.

The 6x4's big brother is the '8x4', sometimes colloquially known as an 'eight-legger', where not only is there two sets of driving wheels but two steering axles at the front offering more positive control over slippery and loose surfaces. The first British rigid eight-legger was Sentinel's DG8 steam wagon launched in 1929.

Finally, the '6x2 Twin-Steer' was a development of the 8x4. It had six wheels, two driven at the rear and four at the front for steering, and in Britain the type was often nicknamed a 'Chinese Six'.

Of course placing all the lorries ever produced into these four types would be impossible on a practical level as there were always going to be anomalies. Many eight-wheeler rigids, for example, could be classed as '8x2' with only one driving axle at the rear, but as the tonnage of loads increased, so did the need for better traction.

BELOW 1948 ERF C1561S 'Chinese Six' 6x2 rigid

Chapter 6

After the Crash

BELOW Mechanical Horses were not always articulated – this 3-ton rigid recreation uses parts of another condemned vehicle and represents a model of the 1930s that Scammell marketed as the Trivan

The devastating effects of the Wall Street Crash were far-reaching. By December 1930, unemployment in Britain had reached 2,500,000 – the parts worst hit being Northern England, Scotland and Wales, areas that traditionally relied on heavy industry. Every class of society in all countries around the globe were dumbfounded by the collapse of the world's economies; destitution was widespread and businessmen who could not even afford to pay wages were targeted; others were left distrusting of theirs and neighbouring state governments. Extremist movements began challenging the system and those left penniless and ruined rallied to the cause.

For Europe, the next ten years would be remembered as a time when the most brutal, terrifying and hated political regime of modern history emerged as an almost unstoppable power. Whilst the people of Britain attempted to recover from financial catastrophe as a result of events in America during October 1929, they kept a nervous watch on the growing tension in countries that bordered Germany – nations that would almost certainly be ill-equipped to defend themselves if there was ever an invasion. And after all, Britain was then

only twenty or so miles across the water.

Within a year of the Crash, a number of British engineering firms including those in the truck industry were beginning to feel the pinch. Orders for new vehicles were evaporating and if your company was not regarded as one of the elite, there was a real risk of bankruptcy. And so it was for Bean Cars of Tipton in Worcestershire and Vulcan of Southport. To be fair Bean had, without realising it, been producing and selling vehicles at a loss, their cars in particular earning a reputation for unreliability, and only four years earlier Bean had been the subject of a takeover bid in light, it is said, of unpaid bills.

Their catalogues consisted of family cars and light trucks and in the financial climate of 1930, the company's owners, Hadfields Steel Foundry, decided to downsize and concentrate exclusively on the commercial vehicle market.

ABOVE A 1930 Gilford AS6 4,000cc van in Danish Bacon Company Ltd livery. Gilfords were built at High Wycombe between 1926 and 1937. This vehicle is the only known survivor of the marque

LEFT This Foden S4 was constructed a year before the last steam wagons left Elworth Works. The Sandbach company finally conceded that the future lay in diesel powered lorries

ABOVE This is the first lorry built by E.R. Foden & Son in 1933. Soon after, the company shortened its name to ERF

A 4-ton goods chassis called the Empire was planned but before it left the drawing board Bean Cars went into liquidation. It was only when they reformed in 1934 as Bean Industries – component suppliers – that the management could properly structure the company and start making a profit.

Peerless were another casualty and although their vehicles looked good on paper, it seemed that potential customers were just not forthcoming. In 1933, the company reverted back to its original business, simply as an agent

for American trucks only this time they were Studebaker.

Foden had embarked on a new era. Finally turning their back on steam wagon production, an area of expertise where they had comfortably earned respect from their peers, the company from Elworth Works in Sandbach had to forge a reputation for building reliable internal-combustion engine vehicles, almost from scratch and several petrol prototypes were made. This had to be done fairly rapidly as they would for the first few years and possibly for many years to come be constantly compared to their (both technically and geographically) nearest rival, the breakaway concern of E.R. Foden & Son Diesel, no more than a mile up the road.

Rather than waste time honing the technical aspects to an acceptable level, ERF as they would soon be known, decided to buy proven mechanicals such as engine and gearbox as off-the-shelf items. This allowed them to quickly get assembly lines up and running, and start trading.

The first ERF, was given the designation C.I.4.4 to indicate that it was a four-wheel vehicle powered by a four-cylinder engine (in this case one of the

ABOVE Dennis 24.8hp 700 gallon tanker supplied new to BP in 1935

tried and tested Gardner 4LWs) of compressed ignition – using the increased temperature of compression to ignite the fuel – or in layman terms, a diesel. It was displayed at the 1933 Olympia Motor Show and having attracted a lot of interest, ERF were soon receiving a regular stream of orders. The drawing office rapidly sketched out plans for other vehicles in the range so that they could tap into a wider market.

A year later, Foden's last steam wagon left the works and all engineering skilled staff were steered towards the new venture. With no member of the original family left on the Board of Directors, Edwin's brother, William was asked to return from his adopted home of Australia and take the reins. By the mid-1930s, Foden had a range of vehicles to rival any of the manufacturers let alone their Sandbach neighbours, including rigid fours, sixes and eights plus articulated sets.

In years gone by, Foden's main rival would have been Sentinel who in the 1930s were still reluctant to accept that the steam wagon's day was about to come to an end. They did, however, take over Henry Garner Ltd in September 1933 who, only two years previous, had begun building a 3, 4 and 6 ton range of '4JO' forward-control diesel and petrol trucks. Garner's production line was moved from the Moseley Motor Works in Birmingham and relocated in Shrewsbury. By 1935, the catalogue had been updated and 3, 4 and 5 ton trucks were being marketed under the Sentinel-Garner banner. Customers had the choice of petrol or diesel power and the engines were shipped into the works from Austin, Meadows or Perkins. Steam wagon production continued alongside but in a much reduced capacity. In December 1936, one of Sentinel's major shareholders and original company founder, Stephen Alley, sold up but in so doing put the company at risk of bankruptcy. To settle outstanding debts, the Garner concern was put up for sale and was purchased by a group of engineers who had previously worked for Dodge Brothers at Kew. Once again Garner assets were moved and preparations were quickly made to restart production in Willesden. A year later the first new Garners were available and were manufactured until the outbreak of war.

In 1931, Ford opened their

BELOW 1936 Vulcan flat-bed lorry completes the HCVS London to Brighton Run sixty years later

ABOVE 1937 Fordson Type 79, built to an American design and assembled in Dagenham

Dagenham works where a new range of commercial vehicles was launched with Ford Thames branding. This was done to differentiate them from anything made at the former Trafford Park facility in Manchester or indeed any other of Ford's production sites.

From 1935, Fordson promoted the Tug, a spindly looking three-wheeler with a cab that took styling cues from the Ford Y Type family saloon. The Tug had a number of applications for example as a small tractor unit, pick-up or delivery van and was available to carry either 3 or 4-ton payloads. It was not as large as the Scammell Mechanical Horse but looked a little more comfortable than Karrier's rather utilitarian Cob.

LYONS TEA

LYONS TEA

J. LYONS & Cº LTD
CADBY HALL
LONDON W14

1936 COMMER VAN
Reg. No. DLU 782

Built during November 1936
and used by Lyons' Gloucester
Depot until the late 1940's.
Restored in 1974, it has since
attended many rallies and was also
used in the T.V. programme
Pennies from Heaven.
Restored again by our own staff
during 1988.

ABOVE This 1937 Commer N starred in Dennis Potter's BBC television series Pennies From Heaven

Only 111 examples were made and all at County Commercial Cars Ltd in Fleet, Hampshire.

In the early-1930s, much of Karrier's work centred around the Cob three-wheeler but in 1932, they announced the 12-ton Colossus six-wheeler. The new model, however, did little to reverse Karrier's falling sales and two years later, they called in the receivers. Rescue came in the form of Humber

Ltd and Karrier joined the growing number of truck subsidiaries within the Rootes Group portfolio. Commer came within Rootes administration and as part of a rationalisation scheme, Karrier production ceased in Huddersfield and moved south to Commer's Luton plant. Where Commer continued manufacturing light to medium category lorries, Karrier were instructed to concentrate their efforts on vehicles destined for the municipal market and a new model, the Bantam was launched in 1935. The Bantam and larger Gamecock would later become the firm's most popular sellers especially after the war when they were built for a wide variety of uses sharing chassis, mechanicals and body parts with their respective Commer equivalent.

The decade had not started so well for Guy Motors after an attempt to break into automobile manufacture with the purchase of the Star Motor Company Ltd had failed. Throughout the following years they concentrated on building the Wolf, Vixen and Otter models which from 1934, would each be graced with a beautifully sculpted American Indian head radiator mascot with the slogan 'Feathers in our Cap'. By the late 1930s, however, the British government, sensing unrest in Central Europe began a program of rearmament and the Guy factory was commandeered to assist.

Alongside the range of trucks aimed at the domestic market, AEC had launched a new 4x2 heavy haulage tractor 4x2 called the Matador. When Britain went to war, this model would become one of the most celebrated vehicles of the campaign. Another AEC product was the Mammoth Major 8, representing the first mass-produced internal-combustion engine eight-wheeler in Britain. It was not long before other companies were offering similar vehicles and in the same year, Leyland launched the Octopus, whilst a little later, Scammell entered the fray with their 'Rigid 8' and Maudslay with the Mikado.

BELOW 1934 Shelvoke & Drewry 15.8hp dustcart on the 1995 HCVS London to Brighton Run

ABOVE 1936 Guy Wolf ambulance featuring the famous American Indian radiator mascot

looking to specialist makers to provide standard units, and Gardner, Dorman and Perkins were all well regarded. During and after the war it was quite a different matter and AEC especially would provide a huge amount of engines for military and domestic use. In Columbus, Indiana, Cummins were perfecting their Model H diesel unit and after the war, a vast number of commercial vehicles on Britain's roads were powered by Cummins engines made in their first factory outside America located at Shotts, North Lanarkshire.

The 1930s saw Morris Commercial expand its range and take up residence at Adderley Park, the former Birmingham home of Wolseley. The Morris catalogue depicted some robust looking workhorses in bonneted and semi-forward-control guises. The Leader and Equiload were especially sturdy beasts but because neither was of a particularly glamorous nature, few examples survived into preservation.

Albion were another firm who specialised in unfussy no-frills transport with four, six and even an eight-wheeler model on offer. The KL 127 was possibly their best selling pre-war type with its no-nonsense slab sided cab. When

At the time, Six-wheelers were popular sellers and models such as the Armstrong-Saurer Dominant, Crossley Atlas, Leyland Beaver (Chinese six) and Rhino, Maudslay Maharaja and Pagefield's Pegasix and Plantagenet afforded a wide choice of vehicle both in 6x2 and double-drive 6x4 configuration.

There were few lorry manufacturers who had the testing facilities or funds to develop their own engines with many

ABOVE 1934 Morris Commercial C Type 30cwt drop-side truck

war broke out in 1939, a number of KL 127s were commandeered into various transport regiments.

A similar range of vehicles to Albion's was being offered by Atkinson who in 1935 needed space to expand and found it on a site in Marsh Lane, Preston. Lacre Lorries Ltd relocated around the same time and seemed to have a thing for garden cities, moving from Letchworth south to Welwyn a year later.

Between 1929 and 1931, all vehicles built at Bedford's Luton plant were marketed as Chevrolet Bedford, but when the W Type went on sale, it heralded the first use of the Bedford name in its own right. The W remained practically unchanged until 1938 when body panels from the popular O Series albeit still retaining the original cab brought it up-to-date and in line with the corporate look then in production. Some of the most stylish vehicles of the period were built on the O derived chassis, epitomised by the beautifully proportioned OB Duple Vista buses, most of which were built in the post-war years.

Towards the end of the 1920s, the Chrysler Corporation bought the Dodge Brothers Company and with it Dodge Bros. (Britain) Ltd. Petrol engines were shipped to Britain for installation into the trucks then built at Kew in Surrey. It was not until 1938, that the practice of importing engines was stopped in favour of using British built Perkins Diesels.

Newcomers in the 1930s included Manchester neighbours Foster and Seddon Ltd and Crossley Motors Ltd.

Foster & Seddon of Salford were initially set up as a road haulage firm in the late 1930s but realised there was a gap in the market for light-weight delivery trucks that did not have to adhere to the 20mph speed limit that anything weighing over 2½ tons was restricted to. Production was sporadic, however, and only really got going in 1947 under the guise Seddon Lorries when the larger Woodstock factory was opened in Oldham.

Although, Crossley had been building automobiles in Gorton for 28 years, the company only commenced dedicated civilian truck production in 1932. In time, they

BELOW This 1937 Albion KL 127 was still in regular use as a coal lorry when pictured at the 1993 Netley Marsh Steam Rally

would become more well-known for their passenger vehicles and by 1937 had given up competing within the car industry altogether. For the time being their catalogue included the 6x4 Atlas for 12-ton payloads.

When the 1930s came to a close, several names had once again fallen by the wayside. Beardmore Engineering of Paisley were better known for their taxi cab range but in 1933 an ancillary factory was put into operation just over five miles north in Dalmuir where truck production commenced. The venture did not turn out to be a great success and was abandoned in less than four years.

The fortunes of steam wagon maker Yorkshire had looked promising and, like fellow 'undertype' builders Sentinel, had tried to adopt the internal-combustion engine for their vehicles. Alongside

their traditional products were a range of Dorman and Gardner-powered diesel lorries ranging from four, six and eight wheelers of between 4 to 15 tons payloads. But by the time Britain and her European neighbours were embroiled in the bloodiest conflict in history, Yorkshire were no longer a commercial vehicle manufacturer.

ABOVE The most recognisable version of the Bedford O chassis was under the fluid lines of the OB coach body. This nicely restored example carries Isle of Wight Southern Vectis livery

Chapter 7

World War II

World War II was the most widespread conflict in history involving over 100 million military personnel and causing the deaths of over 70 million people. Between 1939 and 1942, the Axis powers were able to advance on all fronts conquering most of Europe and Scandinavia. Under intense pressure, countries collapsed and surrendered and with immediate effect came under the control of Hitler's Nazi-governed Germany in the northern regions and Mussolini's Fascist Italy to the south. With only 21 miles of Dover Strait separating the Kent coastline from occupied Calais, it was imperative that first and foremost, the British had to defend their shores, and secondly help rid Britain's European allies of the Axis forces. The Battle of Britain was the prequel to Hitler's planned invasion and to sustain supply levels to the Armed Forces, practically all engineering factories were requisitioned for essential war work.

In Preston, Lancashire, Leyland Motors commenced production of Cromwell tanks alongside its Hippo and Retriever truck models. Their association with the British armed forces would continue after the war with Centurion tank manufacture. Elsewhere, the Pagefield Iron Works in Wigan stopped building trucks and turned their attention to the fabrication of artillery shells. They were also one of the firms to make special cranes and sections for the remarkable Mulberry harbour that in 1944 was towed across the English Channel and assembled off the coast of Normandy as part of the D-Day invasion.

North of the border Albion Motors were commandeered not only into

producing tank transporters but also Enfield No.2 Mk.1 revolvers and by 1945 had provided 24,000 hand guns to the Allied Forces.

Tilling-Stevens' wartime speciality was lorry-mounted searchlights. Indeed after the war, the company was sold to the Rootes Group and no more vehicles were built at Maidstone, focussing instead on developing engines and bodywork construction.

ABOVE A Morris Commercial Quad leads a convoy of military vehicles to the Plymouth Hoe Rally in 1996

Military convoys often contained a variety of artillery units and different trucks were designed to tow certain types of weaponry.

For the main British field guns, the Ordnance QF 18 and 25 pounders and the 4.5 inch howitzer, Morris Commercial constructed the C8 FAT (Field Artillery Tractor), more commonly known as the Quad. This was a short-wheelbase unit actually designed before the conflicts to replace an existing model then used by the military.

By 1945, over 10,000 had been

pressed into service. Meanwhile in Wolverhampton, Guy Motors were making a similar vehicle called the Quad Ant with over 100 chassis specially adapted to carry armoured car superstructure.

AEC's Matador found favour with the Royal Artillery essentially as a 4x4 tractor unit for hauling the 5.5inch Medium or QF 3.75inch anti-aircraft gun. It was built with a forward-control cab of steel sheet over an ash frame and a high ground clearance making it ideal for covering rough terrain. With a 10-ton payload capacity, it had enough space for an artillery crew, ammunition and all the associated equipment. The Matador was powered by AEC's own 7.6 litre diesel engine and could reach speeds in excess of 30mph. It was also well suited to overcoming soft ground such as the desert regions of North Africa and particularly adept at rescuing vehicles stranded in the sand.

ABOVE This 1942 Scammell 6x4 Pioneer recovery truck was pictured at the 1995 Great Dorset Steam Fair

RIGHT The Bedford
QL represented the
British Armed Forces
main cargo lorry and
over 50,000 examples
were built

In six-wheeled Type A form, the
Royal Air Force used Matadors as fuel
bowsers and after the war, a number of the 9,620 Matadors produced
continued to perform sterling work as
recovery trucks.

Providing vehicle support to
the Army's Heavy Regiments was
Scammell's Pioneer of which more
than 750 examples were made. It had a
6x4 configuration and under the bonnet was a 6-cylinder Gardner diesel
engine producing 104bhp. The Pioneer
was particularly effective for towing
the cumbersome 7.2 inch howitzer and
when surplus stocks were sold off in the
late-1940s, many found new owners
among heavy haulage contractors.

One of the largest providers of military trucks was Vauxhall's commercial
vehicle subsidiary, Bedford, who in six
years out-shopped a staggering quarter
of a million vehicles including tanks
and armoured personnel carriers. The
3,519cc 6-cylinder petrol-engine QL
represented the British Armed Forces
main cargo lorry and around 52,250
entered service.

Well-known sports car marque,
Jensen, had diversified in the 1930s with
a small experimental articulated truck.

As the 1,172cc Ford side-valve engine
Jen-Tug, it only went into production
after the war. For now though, the West
Bromwich factory was engrossed in the
production of tank turrets.

Out of the 15,000 vehicles built by
Thornycroft between 1939 and 1945,
around 200 were Terrapins – probably
the most interesting project undertaken
by any of the truck manufacturers during the Second World War. In 1942, sup-

respective side with steering via a lever operated braking system. The front and rear wheel sets were positioned higher off the ground for traversing undulating terrain. The Terrapin came into its own with Operation Switchback during the Battle of Scheldt in late-1944, helping the Canadian 3rd Division stage a successful pincer movement on German forces defending the Leopold and Schipdonk Canals.

Dennis Brothers' expertise in the production of fire appliances would prove crucial to Britain's city fire brigades. During the Blitz of 1940 and 1941, the industrial heartland of Birmingham, Belfast, Sheffield, Glasgow and Manchester, as well as the sea ports of Bristol, Cardiff, Hull Liverpool, Plymouth and Southampton and, of course, London were targeted by the German Luftwaffe. One of the worst affected areas was Coventry and Maudslay who were commissioned to build various components for both ground and air warfare were forced to relocate most of the work out from harms way.

plies of the American-built amphibious DUKWs (colloquially known as Army Ducks) were becoming dangerously short and the British Government commissioned Thornycroft of Basingstoke to design a British equivalent. This was an eight-wheeled armoured personnel carrier powered by two Ford V8 engines mounted side-by-side. Each engine drove a propeller at the back for water propulsion and the four wheels on its

A 'shadow' factory was set up 17 miles south-west at Great Alne between Stratford-on-Avon and Redditch and christened Castle Maudslay. Great Alne railway station was used only by workers travelling down from the city whilst a reduced workforce remained at the Coventry site. On 14th November 1940 came the first bombing raid and on that night alone, the city centre was completely devastated. Other companies providing essential equipment towards the war effort were Lacre and Dodge whose staff numbered many women drafted in to help with the construction of aeroplanes.

At Austin's Longbridge plant, the K series chassis was being made in vast quantities. The K would become the standard basis for ambulances and other emergency vehicles, especially those serving the numerous airfields and landing strips dotted around southern and eastern England.

To enable all vital mass production to continue unabated, there was a constant need for raw materials, not least with the supply of timber, and several firms such as Unipower dedicated their skills towards all-wheel-drive tractors specifically designed for forestry work. Unipower had taken an idea developed by the French truck manufacturer, Latil, and launched their own powerful 4x4 tractor in 1937 but this and vehicles like it would endure long into the next few decades when eventually coming under private ownership. There were also those firms who were allowed to continue civilian vehicle production so that on home territory, at least, some level of normality – loosely speaking – could prevail. Atkinson, Commer and ERF all offered a range of basic workaday vehicles of pre-1939 design that would also initially form the basis of mass-produced civilian trucks, once the war was over.

ABOVE During World War II, Unipower of Perivale, Middlesex built all-wheel-drive tractors specifically for timber work

LEFT This 1942 Austin K2 fire tender was operated by Burton Upon Trent Fire Brigade

ABOVE The 1940 Bedford MWD pick-up and the 1943 Morris Commercial C4 radio truck were both converted to breakdown trucks in the years following World War II

And with practically all diesel engines from specialist manufacturers having been requisitioned by the military, it was left to the large truck producers such as AEC to supply units for civilian use. Unfortunately, paint materials were in demand elsewhere and the bright and gay lorry colour schemes that so defined the vogue of the 1920s and 30s had, for the time being, all but been forgotten. The gloomy mood was further compounded by blackout conditions which stipulated that headlamps should be fitted with slatted masks to cut out ambient light avoiding detection by enemy aircraft. In addition, any vehicle extremities such as mudguards and running boards were painted white to make them more discernible to other night-time drivers crawling along at a snail's pace whilst peering through the darkness.

With Germany occupying most of Europe from 1939 and threatening to cross the English Channel, Britain as a nation stood alone against the enemy forces. The engineering industries were at breaking point trying to produce

essential supplies for the Allies in their attempt to stem the tide. Once again, the government was obliged to ask the United States for help and very soon there came another American invasion. In addition to British trucks, tanks and personnel carriers, more than three million vehicles produced in the United States saw service in all theatres of war and many of them ended up in this country when peace resumed.

ABOVE When war ended, this Bedford OY 3-ton drop-side truck was used by British Railways Midland Region

Chapter 8

The Heyday of the British-built Truck

The Heyday of the British-built Truck World War II ruined Britain's economy and the population began to

suffer from rising prices, regular power cuts, and with many families displaced as a result of the bombing, there was a severe shortage of housing. The jubilation surrounding VE Day was, for the majority, relatively short-lived with the realisation that food rationing would continue for several more years.

In 1948, the newly-elected Labour Government swept in a program of nationalisation that would help some of the most important industries and organisations. Coal mining, amenities such as gas and electricity, iron and steel production and the Bank of England all came under state control. The National Health Service was created providing free medical and dental treatment for all, and Britain's road, rail and canal infrastructure was centralised and integrated by the British Transport Commission. The Big Four railway companies as well as all privately owned wagons were amalgamated under British Rail whilst canals and navigable rivers came under the banner British Waterways. Bus companies such as Bristol Tramways, the British Electric Traction Group, Eastern Coach Works, the London Passenger Transport Board, Midland General and the Tilling Group, as well 246 road haulage firms all passed into one holding although freight carriers under the title British Road Services or BRS would be made separate entities

the following year. Each profit making sector could subsidise those that were either struggling or traditionally relied on public and private donation, and the British economy began to stabilise.

ABOVE Fordson Thames ET6 recovery truck

LEFT A pair of Bristols in British Road Services livery at the 1997 Severn Valley Railway Road/Rail gathering

FAR LEFT A 1949 Guy Wolf in John Lewis colours passes the Pavilion on the 1998 HCVS London to Brighton Run

THE HEYDAY OF THE BRITISH-BUILT TRUCK

The post-war truck industry was beset with problems, not least because of the amount of surplus military vehicles flooding the commercial market. With the sudden escalation in the number of trucks, both large and small businesses of the late-1940s/early-1950s were able buy much needed transport on the cheap as redundant stock was dispersed by the government. History was repeating itself and the Military were simply doing as their 1920s predecessors had done after World War I.

When it came to manufacturing utilitarian transport for the war effort, all thoughts were to keep Britain mobilised during those dark days and understandably vehicles possessed little or no styling. In those desperate times, new, sophisticated or chic design would rarely represent anything more than flights of fancy or doodles on the back of a cigarette packet. Manufacturers such as Albion, Bedford and Ford dusted off their mothballed pre-war plans and with cursory modification commenced construction anew, just to get production moving again.

Throughout the motor industry those involved with lorry production were, it seems, quickest to get going after the conflicts as, of course, haulage of bulk commodities was essential for the recovery of the country's economy. Development over the next ten years was steady rather than spectacular but with the relaxation of certain legislation with regards to the 'Construction and Use' of such vehicles, many companies increased the

BELOW This 3-ton drop-side lorry was exhibited by Jensen at the 1951 Festival of Britain

width, length and the weight carrying potential of some models. This in turn forced local authorities to look into road improvements to cope with the changes.

As the only truck manufacturer to come under the newly nationalised BRS organisation, Bristol were tasked with building a standard heavy goods vehicle that could be distributed to the various BRS depots around the country. This would make maintenance and the supply of replacement parts easier, more convenient and above all cost effective. By 1952, Bristol's development team had won government approval for a 22-ton rigid eight and a 24-ton articulated set.

ABOVE A 1948 AEC Monarch nicely matched to a 1950 Dyson trailer

THE HEYDAY OF THE BRITISH-BUILT TRUCK

BELOW The AEC Militant was launched in 1952 and remained the British Army's tank transporter for more than twenty years. This Mk3 example dates from 1970 and is fitted with a winch capable of pulling 15 tons and a crane that can lift 5 tons

For most people, the 1950s began quite unremarkably. Rationing was still in operation and would not be completely lifted until 1954. There was still an air of austerity across the nation and most vehicles on the road were of pre-war design. But the decade would see some significant changes, not least the opening of the first of a network of motorways – high-speed links between towns and cities that further encouraged the transition of freight carried by rail to goods haulage on the road. In the first five years after VE Day, commercial vehicle numbers rose by half so that by 1952, there were around a million vans, lorries and heavy trucks plying their trade across Britain.

The labour-intensive steam lorry had by now all but vanished from the scene. Even the last surviving devotee, Sentinel of Shrewsbury, had unveiled their first petrol-engine lorry in 1945. A year later, the 4/4DV 7/8-ton four-wheeler was launched with a 5,780cc indirect-injection diesel unit of the company's own design. A tractor unit debuted in 1949 with a larger capacity engine which was quickly following by a six-wheeled chassis in 1950, these being the 4/6DV 4-cylinder and the 6/6 DV 6-cylinder. The Sentinel catalogue was gradually added to with improvements to diesel technology that included a direct-injection engine, but by the middle of the decade, the company was struggling to make ends meet. In 1955 they were the subject of a takeover bid by the Warrington-based North Cheshire Motors Ltd who reformed the truck side of the organisation as Transport Vehicles (Warrington) or TVW – the steam engine department going to Rolls-Royce. The TVW venture was short-lived and, with only

sporadic production over the next five years, the Sentinel wagon legacy finally ended in 1961.

In 1948, AEC took control of both the Maudslay Motor Company and Crossley Motors although, under the all-encompassing umbrella of Associated Commercial Vehicles or ACV, the Maudslay brand was dropped.

Crossley continued but after 1951 only in the capacity of a bus builder at the former World War II aircraft factory at Erwood Park. In 1958, the Crossley company was effectively mothballed and would not appear again until 1969.

THE HEYDAY OF THE BRITISH-BUILT TRUCK

By then ACV had been in the ownership of old rivals Leyland Motors for seven years and Leyland were looking for a registered company for their new bus venture. Realising that Crossley were, to all intents and purposes, still officially trading, they changed the name to Leyland National and embarked on a thirteen-year program where nearly 8,000 buses were completed. This subsidiary of Leyland was finally wound up in 1992 in the hands of the recently-privatised British Aerospace.

For the 1950s, however, AEC went from strength to strength continuing to introduce updated versions of such

legends of the road as the Matador, Monarch, Mercury, Majestic and Mammoth Major. Nevertheless, the Matador was the first to be replaced when in 1952 the Militant became the British Army's heavy gun tractor though its role would gradually change as large artillery pieces made way for rockets and missiles. Affectionately known as the 'Milly', there were those who viewed it with some disdain, particularly for its lack of power-steering especially noticeable at a crawl, and the slow-revving diesel engine which earned it the nickname, 'Knocker'.

By the late 1940s, Leyland had grown enormously and as part of their continuing program of expansion to keep pace with closest rivals AEC, had made various bids on other well-known manufacturers. Just as Albion's HD range was about to hit the high street in 1951, the Glasgow firm began negotiations with their old Preston-based adversaries, with Scammell being Leyland's next target three years later. Once this firm was safely ensconced under the Leyland umbrella, production for all its subsidiaries was streamlined so that each specialised within a certain sector of the truck market and, therefore, were not

in direct competition with one another. Scammell had introduced the Showtrac, a dual-purpose ballast tractor equipped with a powerful electricity generator that became extremely popular amongst its intended customers, the country's fairground operators. Incredibly, all but one of the eighteen produced lasted well into the 1980s and 90s. With Britain being a nation of sentimental enthusiasts who fastidiously insist on restoring or renovating anything of antiquity, the seventeen surviving Showtracs have all retired to a slower pace within the preservation movement.

ABOVE This 1952 AEC Mammoth Major 3 was originally supplied to W.J. King of Bishop's Lydeard in Somerset

Leyland had recognised Scammell's pedigree retaining their skills for their heavy haulage division. This allowed Scammell to continue production of the 6x6 Explorer, a direct development of their World War II gun tractor, the Pioneer. Their most noted activity of the 1950s came with the introduction of the Highwayman articulated tractor unit which under Leyland's influence was fitted with a conventional fifth wheel coupling. It became one of the Watford-based company's most popular models until phased out in the late-1960s.

In Guildford, Dennis were building the Pax, a small and neat long-bonnet vehicle that could be bought in various guises from tipper truck to articulated brewery dray. Another of their tractor units was the Horla, available with a choice of either their own-design petrol engine (made on the former White & Poppe site) or the ubiquitous Perkins P6 diesel. Dennis, having remained an independently run organisation, had to compete in as many markets as the factory could cope with and offered a whole range of vehicles to cover all needs, from the basic four-wheeler to large rigids and more specialist equipment whilst still providing reliable appliances to fire brigades across the country.

Down in Hampshire, Thornycroft's first post-war models were the Nippy 3-ton, Sturdy 5/6-

BELOW One of the 900 Bedford RLHZs, more commonly known as Green Goddesses that were built for the British civil defence program

ton, Amazon 12-ton and the Trusty 15-ton but a new vehicle was on the drawing board aimed at customers, specifically the Anglo-Persian Oil Company, for the transportation of pipes over rough ground between oilfields in the Middle-East. It was given the name Mighty Antar after Antar Ibn Shadded, a pre-Islamic Arabian hero, and mighty it was! The first batch was each powered by Rover's V8 Meteorite petrol engine, a modified version of the V12 Rolls-Royce Meteor used in the Cromwell tank, but later, a diesel alternative was offered by Rolls-Royce. In 1951, the British Army took delivery of several examples to transport the new Centurion tank. The Army were looking at the Leyland FV 1000 carrier to move the heavier Conqueror but when it was found to be too top heavy, Thornycroft stepped in once more. The Antar found service in a number of European armed forces in articulated tractor or ballast tractor form and some were used as recovery

trucks. So successful was the design that as a tank transporter, the Antar was not fully replaced until 1986 with the launch of Scammell's Commander.

Bedford's 7-ton S Series, the 'Big Bedford' was launched during the early-1950s and allowed the company to tap into new markets.

ABOVE The 'Kleer Vue' cab was designed and built by J.H. Jennings & Sons Ltd. It was first unveiled by ERF in 1952 and was still in use ten years later as seen on this 1962 KV66GX tipper wagon

A development of the S was the four-wheel-drive RL. Yet another vehicle destined for military use, nearly 75,000 RLs would eventually emerge from Bedford's Luton factory. In 1953, the first examples were delivered to the Armed Forces and in the same year, production of the RLHZ Self Propelled Pump commenced as part of Britain's civil defence program. More affectionately known as 'Green Goddesses', RLHZs formed the Auxiliary Fire Service's reserve unit of 900 appliances during an era when it was thought a nuclear attack from the Soviet Union very likely. The official line was that in such an event, there would be an overwhelming need to support the nation's regular fire service. Thankfully, Green Goddesses were never called up to fulfil their intended role and in 1968, were finally put into storage.

Regularly maintained and in perfect working order, they were occasionally brought out of their slumber if, for example, fire-fighters were on strike. In 1994, they were called upon to alleviate severe flooding in Chichester but ten years later, the fleet was deemed surplus to requirement and gradually disposed of. Whilst a large number went into private hands and museums, most examples began new lives in third world countries performing the sort fire-fighting role they would have originally been designed for.

BELOW 1952 Foden FG6/15 drop-side rigid eight

Cheshire, or to be more precise, Sandbach was the home of Foden and ERF. Ever since Edwin Foden had left the family's steam wagon business to help son, Dennis, set up his diesel-engine truck manufacturing facility across town, the two firms had remained rivals. In twenty years, ERF lorries had earned a reputation for quality and reliability. For the 1952 season, ERF introduced a stylish oval radiator grill and during the next few years it graced the cab of a number of new models. One of these was the attractive KV (or Kleer Vue) with its full-width cab and a curved two piece windscreen which made for a light and airy interior and provided superior panoramic vision.

ABOVE In response to ERF's Kleer Vue cab, Foden launched the S.21 glass reinforced plastic cab in 1958. This one is seen on a 1961 KG 6LX rigid eight at the 1994 HCVS Bournemouth to Bath Run

The cab was built by J.H. Jennings & Sons Ltd who occupied space at ERF's Sun Works site on Middlewich Road. In time, this coachbuilder also supplied cabs for Rowe Hillmaster of Liskeard as well as coachbuilding horsebox, removals van and mobile shop bodies and, in 1963, would come under ERF's ownership.

The Rowe-Hillmaster business started off as a coach operator working out of Rowe's Garage in the small Cornish village of Dobwalls. In 1953,

BELOW Atkinson L 1586 4-axle model

proprietor Maurice Rowe decided that there was a niche market for vehicles designed specifically to cope with the demanding hills in the local area. A year later Rowe built a prototype 6/7-ton truck around a Meadows 4DC and encouraged by its performance and the interest it received, sold the family garage and coach operation and entered full production under the banner M.G. Rowe (Motors) Doublebois Ltd. By 1959, the catalogue boasted fourteen different models with a wide choice of power plants made by AEC, Gardner, Leyland or Meadows. After only six years in operation and with debts of £3,000, the banks called in the official receivers and the business was wound up. In total 115 Rowe Hillmaster commercial vehicle chassis were built.

Foden had the engineering know-how to develop their own diesel engines whereas ERF's were all bought in, but not having the luxury of professionally-made cabs on

tap, Foden's range remained conservatively square and even the immediate post-war FG model would quickly look outdated alongside ERF's KV. It was not until the mid-1950s that Foden had something to rival the KV for style with the S.20. In 1958, however, the shapely contours of the S.21's glass reinforced plastic cab set new standards with its ultra-modern lines. Rather unkindly earning the nickname 'Mickey Mouse' by some and 'Spaceship Sputnik' by others, it was certainly one of the most unusual styling exercises to grace a commercial vehicle and to those with at least a modicum of taste, possibly the most attractive of any post-war models.

Over the decade, Atkinson, Bristol and Seddon were just some of the other companies who had also used glass reinforced plastic in cab construction although Seddon had theirs made through a subsidiary called Pennine Coachcraft.

ABOVE Commer Superpoise pick up

a truck than developing, fabricating and rigorously testing in-house designs, both for the company and the customer. In 1957, Atkinson unveiled the Omega, a 333bhp supercharged monster powered by Rolls-Royce's C6.SFL engine. Designed as an articulated tractor unit, Omegas were specifically designed for heavy-haulage work and able to pull around 90 tons over soft terrain. Only seven are believed to have been made.

Seddon, ERF and Rutland were all proud to call themselves assemblers and alongside Atkinson, built up a good customer base with many vehicles being shipped abroad. Seddon moved to Oldham when the war ended and in 1951 became a public company under the guise of Seddon Diesel Vehicles Ltd. With the increase in available factory space, they were able to expand their range considerably and tap into more sectors of the market. With weight limits having been relaxed towards the end of the decade, the 1958 catalogue included a 198bhp Cummins diesel-powered 30-ton 6x4

In 1947, Atkinson had moved from Marsh Lane, Preston to new premises at Winery Lane, Walton-le-Dale. Atkinson were lorry assemblers rather than fabricators and would have a chassis made to their own specification and fitted with proven engine and gearbox bought in. Their preferred choice of the 1950s was either Cummins or Rolls-Royce and towards the end of the decade, Gardner's 150bhp unit. Assembling a vehicle from proprietary items was a more cost effective way of producing

heavy haulage tractor called the Sirdar.

Yet another firm desperate to find larger premises was Commer who in 1953 upped sticks from their Biscot Road site, Luton and made the four mile hop to Dunstable. Since the war, one of Commer's most popular models was the Superpoise not least from 1950 when the S-Type took on styling cues from parent company Humber's automobile range. It had full width bodywork which was becoming more commonplace amongst commercial vehicles of the era, another example being Austin's Loadstar. By the late 1950s, Austin and Morris (Commercial was dropped from their title in 1956) had amalgamated to form the British Motor Corporation or BMC. For a short time, vehicles from both companies shared identical mechanicals, components, and bodywork, but continued to be sold as either Austin or Morris trucks to secure a greater share of the market. It was not long, however, before the Austin and Morris brands were phased out. A major development during the decade saw Swedish giant Volvo introduce the turbocharged diesel engine and it would not be long before the technology had filtered through to British lorry manufacturers.

ABOVE Another vehicle completing the 1995 HCVS London to Brighton Run was this 1950 Austin Loadstar

Chapter 9

The Swinging Sixties

The 1960s was the era of radical thinking, greater individual freedom and youth revolution. It was a time when pop music really came into its own hippies promoted flower power and free love for all. The Vietnam War was at its height and the world held its breath over the Cuban Missile Crisis.

But that would all have to happen without the likes of Garner, Jensen, Maudslay, Pagefield, Rutland, Tilling-Stevens and Vulcan who had between 1945 and 1959, all disappeared from the truck manufacturing world altogether. The decade would also see not only the closure of thousands of miles of railways under Doctor Beeching's 'Reshaping of British Railways' which could only be beneficial to the road haulier, but a huge influx of foreign truck makes. By 1970, the traditional British lorry producer was fighting to keep afloat in an increasingly crowded market and fighting to halt takeover bids from foreign rivals and keep Britain's engineering heritage alive.

During World War II Dennis had earned much respect within the Industry for their expertise in the production of fire appliances, and this

BELOW F107 fire recovery truck at the 1995 Dennis Centenary Rally, Amberley Chalk Pits Museum

work had continued long after peace was declared. The problem was, fire engines, pumps and ladder vehicles were always going to be expensive kit and orders were not as forthcoming as for those firms who manufactured run-of-the-mill commercial vehicles. To cope with the shortfalls and to keep their 1,300 staff in employment, Dennis' activities were certainly varied during the 1960s, specialising in buses and coaches, municipal vehicles such as gully and cesspool emptiers as well as refuse lorries, ambulances and tractors, and even promoted a range of lawn mowers. On the commercial vehicle side, the nimble little Pax, Condor and Heron found many roles in the private sector from flat-bed truck and removals van to fuel tanker and mobile shop.

Rutland is now a long-forgotten make and was only in existence for ten years. A relatively small concern, it was founded in 1947 by Frank Manton of Croydon as an agent for Commer but numerous Rutland-badged vehicles were assembled at his New Addington premises under the company banner Motor Traction. These included the Manton, Toucan, Albatross, Stuka and Eagle models before business closed

towards the end of the decade.

Another firm struggling to stay afloat was Pagefield. The assets of this company had been operated in reduced capacity by Walker & County Cars since 1948 but they in turn closed their doors for the last time in 1966.

ABOVE 1963 Wales & Edwards 'Loadmaster' articulated electric truck

BELOW This Atkinson L1786 was new to Castrol in 1964 and was used to supply oil for power station transformers

Towards the end of the 1950s, Bedford's design team were quietly working on a model that would take the world by storm and remain in production for over twenty years. The Bedford TK was announced at the 1960 Commercial Motor Show to replace the aging S Series and heralded a new era and standard in light and medium truck design. Its introduction was of huge importance to the British commercial vehicle industry, a landmark that prompted all other manufacturers to rethink their production techniques. Available with either 4 or 6-cylinder engines, petrol or diesel, the TK was used in practically all spheres of industry requiring a comfortable, nimble and reliable workhorse. Orders for fleets of TKs were taken in addition to individual purchases and many hundreds saw service within the nationalised industries. Numerous articulated tractor units were operated by British Rail's freight department and special-bodied vehicles called Pole Kings and Polecats were used by British Telecom to erect wooden telegraph poles. The British Army first began using a four-wheel-drive derivative called the MK which

BELOW 1963 ERF 54G SF Sabrina

overlapped with the long-serving RL that was beginning to look decidedly dated. By 1980, nearly 12,000 MKs had been built for military work. They were gradually phased out with the introduction of the higher specification TM of 1974. A larger version called the KM joined the range in 1966 which used a similar cab albeit restyled with twin headlamps and deeper bumpers, a beefed up chassis to cope with payloads of 16-tons and over, and a new and more powerful diesel engine.

The Thames Trader was another vehicle considered at the time to be state-of-the-art. Conceived towards the end of the previous decade, its styling relied heavily on American tastes with full-width cab and snub nose bonnet and when it was first seen on the high street looked completely out of place amongst the amassed lines of traditional British sit-up-and-beg offerings. It was the first vehicle under the Ford Thames banner but after 1965 (the year Trader production ended in favour of the K Series), all commercial vehicles built in Dagenham were branded as Fords.

In that year, Ford also launched the D Series, a serious and subsequently successful challenger to Bedford's TK.

1962 saw the first British truck to feature a mass-produced tilting cab. The Foden S24 was constructed of glass reinforced plastic and gave superior access into the engine bay over a conventional fixed cab. It was not long before rival manufacturers were adopting the idea.

ABOVE The TK went on sale in 1961 and became Bedford's best selling truck. This one dates from 1983

Another glass reinforced plastic cab was featured on the updated Scammell Routeman, Handyman and Trunker and like the Foden S.21 of 1958, broke the mould in terms of individuality. It was created by Giovanni Michelotti, a sports car designer whose earlier work included the Triumph Herald, Spitfire, GT6 and Stag, BMW's 700 series and the elegant lines of the Maserati 3500 GT.

Get Lucky was an album released in 2009 by former Dire Straits front man, Mark Knopfler. One of the tracks entitled Border Reiver, makes reference to one of Albion's best selling lorry models of the 1960s. Indeed, the lyrics include the lines "My Scotstoun Lassie", "She's an Albion" and "Sure as the Sunrise" (the latter alluding to Albion's radiator design introduced in 1928). Mr Knopfler was obviously a fan! Taking its name from a pre-war model, the Reiver along with the Chieftain featured the distinctive stepped-front all pressed steel 'LAD' Vista-Vue cab shared with Leyland's Comet and Scammell's early Trunker model. In only four years, the next generation within the conglomerate were sporting the Ergomatic, Leyland's first forward tilting cab. It was designed with greater attention to driver safety and comfort, and climbing up into the cab was made easier with the entrance steps located ahead of the front wheels, a feature that was also to the benefit of interior space. The Ergomatic was certainly popular with

BELOW The Ford Thames Trader proved a popular choice in the light truck market

fleet operators, so much so that it was still in production right up to the 1980s.

In 1961, Guy Motors amalgamated with the Jaguar Car Company and immediately made changes to the management structure. The sports car makers also invested funds into its new subsidiary bringing welcome relief to the cash-strapped Wolverhampton firm. Jaguar's involvement with Guy was acknowledged in 1964 by lending its initial to the Big J model but in that year, Jaguar merged with BMC to create British Motor Holdings. The Transport Act of 1963 saw a reorganisation of the nationalised road, rail and waterway networks and six years later yet another overhaul of the system saw the introduction of the National Freight Corporation. This was sub-divided into four divisions consisting of British Road Services Ltd, BRS Parcels Ltd, Containerway & Roadferry Ltd and Pickfords.

ABOVE With Bedford's TK taking the lion's share of sales in the first half of the decade, Ford launched the Ford D in 1965 to redress the balance

ABOVE 1969 Atkinson 'Viewline' heavy haulage tractor

in two guises, first with a full width 'grille' most of which was just there for aesthetics, and the other as a more traditional narrow radiator with the large Atkinson Circle A. The latter proved more popular and the Viewline remained in production until the early 1970s. Some versions of the Viewline used the same Cummins V6-200 engine that was installed in Guy's Big J.

Changes were certainly afoot as towards the end of the 1960s, Leyland could list AEC, Albion, Alvis, Crossley, Scammell, Thornycroft, Rover and Standard-Triumph as well as road-roller specialists Aveling-Barford amongst its assets. In 1968, the Leyland Motor Corporation and British Motor Holdings pooled their resources as one huge conglomerate entitled the British Leyland Motor Corporation, boasting nearly forty motor manufacturing sites across the country. The consolidation

In 1966, Atkinson launched the Viewline series. This was particularly distinctive but ungainly looking beast, because of the huge expanse of curved windscreen within the glass reinforced plastic cab that accounted from the top half of the front elevation. It was built

of all parties was done on the advice of the government but many of BLMC's ancillaries were, unfortunately, close to bankruptcy and any available funds were being spread too thinly across the organisation. Whilst BLMC were getting themselves into all sorts of trouble, the Detroit-based Chrysler Corporation were claiming a greater stake in Britain's motor industry by systematically taking over the Rootes Group in stages. By 1967 the deal was complete and eventually there would be a program of rationalisation, but for now, Dodge, Commer and Karrier would be sharing factory floor space in Dunstable.

BELOW On the left is a 1960 ERF KV and on the right is the next generation ERF, a 1974 A Series

Chapter 10

The Final Years

In the 1970s, there was a huge influx of foreign makes that did little to help the fortunes of what was, by now, the last vestiges of a once world-dominating British motor industry. With a greater variety of vehicles available, more and more private businesses, large haulage contractors and those organisations which relied on the work of the humble lorry were factoring comfort, fuel economy and cost when choosing the next addition to their transport fleet.

At the beginning of the decade, haulage specialists, M. Elliott & Sons of West Howe, Bournemouth were operating an assortment of trucks, from rigid flat-beds to curtain-sided articulated lorries, as well as purpose-built semi-trailers for conveying repeat consignments of steel coil and abnormal loads in and out of Poole Docks. One of Elliott's regular drivers, Fred Wood, recalls that almost all new trucks were at one time provided by Foden. This was not unusual, however, for fleet operators often stayed loyal to one make, but as foreign manufacturers infiltrated the British commercial vehicle market, so sample vehicles would be sent out to tempt potential customers to buy.

BELOW The foreign invasion begins! During the 1970s, MANs replaced all the fleet of Fodens operated by Bournemouth hauliers, M. Elliott & Sons

Around 1977, Fred was asked by the management team to evaluate a MAN that had recently been loaned to them via one of the German company's sales reps. Within a few days he was able to report that it was a far superior product in terms of ease of driving, ride comfort and, with its full width wrap-around windscreen, visibility in comparison to the trucks in the Elliott fleet. New Fodens of the late-70s certainly looked staid with outdated split screens, round headlights and square bumpers. By the 1980s, Elliott management had relinquished completely and its entire fleet was made up of trucks built in Munich.

For lorry manufacturers Commer and Karrier, the early-1970s would prove to be the last time their names graced the front of any vehicles under Chrysler's ownership. The 100 Commando Series was Chrysler/Rootes most popular truck on the European market. It had been launched during the previous decade and could be bought as a Commer, Karrier or Dodge. By 1973, Chrysler had assumed full control of the three companies and over the next couple of years began phasing out the Commer and Karrier names. When Chrysler sold the remnants to PSA Peugeot-Citroën

in 1978, only the Dodge brand was in use. Motor Panels were one of the main suppliers of tilt cabs making a standardised design for a number of manufacturers including ERF, Argyle, Seddon and Guy. Once each cab had been delivered to the factory, it was down to the individual company's factory as to how any modicum of distinguishable branding was applied.

BELOW Trucks do not always have to be of colossal proportions! Here is the diminutive Reliant Ant

Argyle Diesel Electronics was a newcomer compared to its contemporaries having only been established in 1970 in East Kilbride. In its three years of operation, it would build only a handful of vehicles, mostly the fairly unremarkable Christina 16-ton four-wheeler. Elsewhere, ERF and Guy were quietly maintaining a steady flow of work while Seddon and Atkinson amalgamated to form Seddon-Atkinson Vehicles. The move was hardly noticeable to all but

the ardent enthusiast as both entities remained separate with regards to their individual styling. Seddon-Atkinson was then the subject of a takeover from International Harvester and with Viewline production ending in 1972, the last Atkinson built largely as an independent concern, was a Defender rigid eight which rolled off the Walton-le-Dale assembly line in 1975. Even though the 'Circle A' was carried on the last of the 'Atkinson' models, the 200, 300 and 400 series, these were all built by committee at Seddon's Oldham factory and marketed as Seddon-Atkinsons. Once again Motor Panels tilt cabs were exploited with International Harvester engines shipped over from the States in addition to units from Perkins and Cummins. In 1986, Seddon-Atkinson was sold to the Spanish group ENASA and under their influence began to share components with the other companies within their portfolio. As an ongoing process of streamlining, Leyland gradually

BELOW A 1977 Leyland Buffalo articulated lorry featuring the Ergomatic cab

ABOVE An Atkinson and a BMC Leyland, both sporting the livery of BRS Parcel Services leave Bournemouth's King's Park on the 1998 HCVS Run

dropped the Albion model names, especially once the Scotstoun factory was decommissioned. Guy Motors was also a victim of the changes and ceased trading in 1978.

The British Leyland Motor Corporation was one of the largest single employees in the country with 31,000 personnel working in the truck sector alone. By the mid-1970s the corporation was running into financial difficulties. In 1975 BLMC filed for bankruptcy which was officially put down to problems with the trade unions, the 1973 OPEC oil crisis, the three-day week and high inflation. In reality there had been very little commitment to serious development and certainly amongst the subsidiaries responsible for family car production, the best models put forward to compete against the likes of Ford Escort and Cortina were the ill-conceived Morris Marina and the remarkably dreadful Austin Allegro. In some desperation, a new company was formed under the control of the government thus creating British Leyland Limited or BL.

THE FINAL YEARS

BELOW Serious heavy haulage at the 2006 Great Dorset Steam Fair. On the left is a 1970 Scammell Contractor ballast tractor and to the right is a 1960 Thornycroft Mighty Antar

In 1978, a sub-group called BLCV was formed to manage BL's commercial vehicle interests and included Leyland Vehicles Limited, Alvis Limited, Coventry Climax Limited and Self Changing Gears Limited.

In Luton, Bedford were also struggling to challenge Ford in light of the recession. In 1981 they had to respond to the launch of the modern-design Ford Cargo, a successor to the D-Series.

Two years later Bedford's TL was announced to replace the outmoded TK. Unfortunately the TL was not as popular as its predecessor and when Bedford failed to win a contract with the MoD to build 4x4 trucks for the Armed Forces, it spelt the end of heavy vehicle production at Luton. Bedford and the Japanese company Isuzu combined in 1986 to build Isuzu MU Wizard and Renault vans with both

Vauxhall and Opel badging. The Bedford name had become redundant and subsequently disappeared from the truck scene. A year later, the old Bedford factory at Dunstable was sold to AWD Ltd who continued to build the TL and its larger sibling, the TM.

Elsewhere Unipower, having forged a niche making an off road 4x4 called the Invader that found favour with the Fire Service, were bought out by AC Cars of Thames Ditton. Subsequently production moved to Surrey and then on to Watford when Scammell's factory came available on closure. That was in 1988, a year after the Leyland Truck division merged with the Dutch company DAF to form DAF NV, and trading as Leyland DAF. In fact throughout the 1980s, there was enormous uncertainty among the staff beneath the BL umbrella as mergers

and divestments took place every few months. One of these had been the closure of AEC's Southall factory ahead of Leyland's new T45 and Constructor range.

ABOVE 1983 Bedford TL recovery truck of Ray Herritts & Sons, Stafford

Shelvoke & Drewry who had been quietly making their Special Purpose Vehicle Pump Ladders, its various derivatives as well as some municipal vehicles, were bought out by the American concern, Dempster Company. Further vehicles were subsequently branded as Shelvoke-Dempster but when SD was sold to another private buyer in the late-1980s, they faced competition from Dennis in the refuse truck market.

By the following decade, Shelvoke was another name to disappear.

At the end of the 1970s, Foden were financially in dire straits and only avoided going into liquidation through large contracts with the Ministry of Defence. PACCAR, the parent organisation of American truck giants Kenworth and Peterbilt stepped in and rescued them and for some peculiar reason, allowed Foden to trade under the name

BELOW 1995 Dennis F88 Rapier of West Sussex Fire Brigade

Sandbach Engineering Company for the next two years. In 1983 they reverted back to some normality under the guise Foden Trucks and launched the up-to-date 2000, 3000 and 4000 series. There seemed to be constant upheaval within the truck industry during the 1980s with National Freight Corporation being one of the first of many state-owned industries to be privatised under Thatcher's Tory government.

In 1986, the Italian Iveco Group took control of Ford UK's truck business. Six years later, Iveco spread its umbrella a little further when it bought out the ENASA Group and its subsidiaries, including a rather diluted Seddon-Atkinson.

Leyland-DAF were declared insolvent in 1993 and through a series of management buy-outs, four separate companies were formed: DAF Trucks of Eindhoven; LDV Limited – a van manufacturer based in Birmingham;

ABOVE Between 1983 and 2002, 125 Scammell Commanders served as tank transporters for the British Army

Multipart Solutions Limited who continued to work out of their previous Chorley premises; and Leyland Trucks. Things were beginning to look positive again as all of a sudden there was a wholly British truck manufacturer once more.

Out of all the British truck manufacturers, ERF remained independent after all the others had been swallowed up by large corporations. They were

BELOW This LDV Convoy was new to Salisbury District Council Environmental Services in 2002

not immune, however, and in 1996 were taken under the wing of Western Star Truck Holdings based in British Columbia, Canada for £27.4 million.

DAF Trucks' independence did not last long either and only three years after going their separate way, PACCAR agreed to buy them out. In no time at all, DAF and Foden were badge engineering similar models, fitting identical steel cabs to their respective trucks.

Foden were beginning to pick up trade within the European market again when the PACCAR group became even larger with takeover of Leyland Trucks in 1998. In a strange twist, Leyland then began supplying delivery lorry cabs to the likes of Kenworth and Peterbilt!

As the new Millennium dawned, only the last few remnants of a once great truck industry remained in Britain. In 2000, the huge German corporation Volkswagen added to an ever expanding portfolio of subsidiaries when its

lorry division, MAN bought ERF from Western Star. MAN then invested around £28 million in a new state-of-the-art factory in Erf Way, Middlewich where for the first time in the company's history, all production and administration would be under one roof. The future was starting to look rosy.

ERF's old adversaries, Foden was just about surviving and launched a new range in 2001 but a year later, MAN put an end to ERF production at Middlewich, one year short of the company's 70th Anniversary, and decided to centralise manufacturing processes to Germany.

ABOVE The foreign invasion continues! There are few lorry manufacturers trading in Britain today and the majority of trucks on our roads such as this enormous Scania 144L are built abroad

BIG BOOK OF TRUCKS

Around the same time, Iveco started to streamline their assets and closed Seddon-Atkinson's Oldham factory.

Foden hung on until 2005 when PACCAR felt that it had one too many brands and after 150 years, the Foden name also disappeared for good. With the Leyland Truck plant concentrat-ing on building DAF trucks, the very last Foden rolled off the Croston Road production line. It did not have to travel far, however, because as a piece of his-tory, it immediately entered the British Commercial Vehicle Museum located on the site of the old King Street works of Leyland Motors.

ABOVE In 2012, this pair of Dennis refuse lorries shared the Christchurch Borough Councils municipal vehicle depot with similar dust carts made by Seddon-Atkinson

LEFT This 2003 Seddon-Atkinson sewage lorry stands forlorn in the pouring rain

Chapter 11

Diesel and ICE

RIGHT 1897 Daimler Canstatt lorry similar to the company's first commercial vehicle built a year earlier

During the mid 19th Century, several inventors set out to construct an engine that could run efficiently and reliably on petrol. It was not until 1867, that Nicolaus August Otto of Cologne was able to patent the first practical four-stroke internal-combustion engine (ICE). In that same year, siblings Francis and William Crossley founded the Manchester-based engineering firm, Crossley Brothers, and began refining Otto's engine design until it was ready to go into production nine years later.

Other inventors were looking at crude oil as a fuel source and by 1890 primitive examples had been made by Priestman Brothers of Hull, George Brayton – an American mechanical engineer living in of Boston, Massachusetts, and Herbert Akroyd-Stuart of Halifax in Yorkshire.

After working with steam engines that ran on ammonia vapour, French-born German inventor, Rudolf Christian Karl Diesel published an essay entitled Theory and Construction of a Rational Heat-engine to Replace the Steam Engine and Combustion Engines Known Today. Heinrich von Buz, director at MAN AG allowed Diesel to test his theories in the company's Munich workshops and in 1892, Diesel filed for a patent for his compression-ignition engine design.

It needed to be more robustly-constructed than a petrol engine due to the greater forces being exerted within the piston chamber and,

because of the increased weight, was not deemed suitable for certain applications such as aircraft propulsion. Indeed it would not be a common power unit for heavy commercial vehicles until the 1930s.

RIGHT 1924 Tilling-Stevens TS3A petrol-electric flat-bed truck

The accolade for building the first internal-combustion engine truck intended for serious production goes to the Daimler Motoren Gesellschaft of Bad Canstatt, Germany. Having already built the world's first motorcycle called the Reitwagen (riding wagon) in 1885, Gottlieb Daimler embarked on perfecting the petrol engine, powering a series of autocars that represented little more than crude motorised carriages. By the mid-1890s, however, his vehicles were more sophisticated and when the Phoenix was announced in 1897, it featured chain drive from the front-mounted optional 2 or 4-cylinder engine, a four-speed gearbox and a choice of bodywork. This included a forward-control open wagon – a lightweight and useful alternative to the horse and cart.

In this country, John Thornycroft was one of the first manufacturers to build a petrol-engine vehicle when, in 1902, he completed a 4-ton experimental truck. Three years later, the first production run of sixteen identical petrol-engine chassis were constructed at the Lancashire Steam Motor Company in Leyland.

At about the same time, W.A. Stevens of Maidstone in Kent was developing a petrol-electric vehicle where the engine generated enough electricity to power motors to drive the road wheels.

Thornycroft's company prided itself on the construction of reliable steam engines but in 1907 switched completely to the manufacture of internal-combustion engines. In 1925, Leyland began experimenting with a prototype diesel engine. They were already manufacturing petrol units and for the time being, it was clear that these would eventually supersede steam as universally used motive power.

A year later Leyland called a halt to steam wagon production. Other companies were showing interest in diesel power and by the end of the decade, Britain's first truck had been put into production at Kerr Stuart's Stoke-on-Trent factory. This was a 6-ton forward control vehicle with a 6-cylinder Helios diesel engine.

In 1930, Leyland exhibited its first direct-injection diesel truck at the Olympia Motor Show and three years later, the company embarked on full production.

Chapter 12

From Functionality to Style - The Evolution of the Cab

When Gottlieb Daimler built the first truck in 1897, there was no real precedent as to how a motorised goods-carrying 'lurry' should look so it was only natural to adapt existing practice from the horse-drawn cart. Early commercial vehicles were therefore largely primitive affairs with little or no wet weather protection unless an operator was kind enough to invest in a leather apron to shield the driver's legs. But there was still little consideration given to safety. Perched on top of the driver's seat, open to the elements, an operator was forever in danger if the vehicle were to overturn. It was several years before any attempt was made to improve, at the very least, driver comfort when wooden-framed folding canvas roofs were introduced affording weather protection from above or behind. It was rare, even up to

World War I, for a lorry manufacturer to include side screens and only in the 1920s did glazed entrance doors become more widely used.

By the mid-1930s, enlarged cabs containing sleeping accommodation for the driver were being introduced in greater numbers in America. The first company to trial them was Kenworth, a company incorporated only ten years earlier by Harry Kent and Edgar Worthington.

Around the same time as the emergence of the sleeper cab, American manufacturers were building 'cab-over' trucks. In Britain these are called 'forward control' where the driving position is over the front axle and engine. For a long time, forward control cabs were the preferred choice of haulage operator in Britain and Europe where there were stringent rules regarding overall vehicle length. They were not as popular with truck mechanics as the engine was very difficult to reach.

LEFT 1917 Albion Model LX 4-ton lorry with forward-control or 'overtype' cab, 1996 Plymouth Hoe Rally

FAR LEFT This four-wheel horse-drawn wagon on display at the Severn Valley Railway's Bewdley Station shows the rudimentary protection afforded to its driver by way of a hooped canvas cover

In 1951, Commer's QX model was fitted with such a cab and access to the 6-cylinder petrol unit was through a hatch in the floor. A handy feature of the QX was the positioning of the driver and passenger doors ahead of the wheel arches. This meant that the seat was less of an obstruction and the gap through the open doorway was larger to step up and into.

BELOW 1958 Commer QX forward-control tipper truck

The problem of easy engine access, however, was solved with the invention of the 'tilt cab' where the whole driving compartment pitched forward, hinged close to the front bumper. The first production tilt cab in Britain featured on the 1962 Foden S24.

Some driving cabs, especially on mobile cranes and airport crash tenders are situated above a protruding overhang allowing the vehicle wheelbase to be shorter thus aiding manoeuvrability. In the United States, this type is referred to as a 'cab-over-in-front'.

The most common alternative to the 'forward control' is the 'normal control' or 'bonnet' type, which as the term suggests features a bonnet ahead of the driving position containing the engine. This configuration is commonly used in The States where legislation on truck length is not so restricting and Americans generally refer to it as the 'conventional' type.

A slight variation on both

ABOVE This 1952 'parrot-nosed' Dodge Kew was attending the 1997 HCVS Bournemouth to Bath Run

'forward control' and 'bonnet' types, is the 'semi forward control' where the rearmost part of the engine encroaches into the cab between the driver and passenger seats.

Right up to the late-1940s, any curvature to the cab bodywork, such as those around the edges of the roof line or indeed the mudguards, would have been panel beaten by hand or at best machine rolled by eye to form the desired profile and right up to the late 1940s, lorry cabs were typically boxy affairs. Across the Atlantic,

however, it was a very different story and ideas filtering in from the United States would largely influence the way designers styled the British truck cab in the coming years. This was illustrated none more so than by a cab made in the 1950s by coachbuilders, Briggs Motor Bodies Limited. Earning the unfortunate nickname 'parrot-nose' on account of its ogee-curved combined-bonnet and radiator-venting panels, protruding forward of the full-width and tastefully profiled wings, it was available as an off-the-shelf item.

It was used on the Dodge 100, Fordson Thames ET6 and Leyland Comet representing an early form of 'badge-engineering' and giving potential purchasers the preferred choice of mechanicals but cloaked beneath a fashionable body shared by other marques.

Another development, again swayed by American practice, was the placement of headlights within the wheel mudguards. Prior to that, separate lamp units were attached almost as an after-thought to the cycle wings of bonneted trucks or, in the case of forward-control lorries, to the front of the cab.

During the 1950s, a number of truck producers were making use of glass reinforced plastic for cab and body panelling. One of the first British manufacturers to embrace this lightweight material was Seddon Diesel Vehicles Ltd. Others soon followed suit such as Bristol in 1955, and Foden, Atkinson and Scammell in 1958. The Atkinson MkI cab featured a two-part wrap-around windscreen which, apart from the vertical centre line, gave superior visibility over its predecessors. On the 1962 Scammell Routeman II, the Giovanni Michelloti-designed cab really pushed the boundaries and showed what could be achieved with glass reinforced plastic moulding techniques.

BELOW The stylish Giovanni Michelloti-designed Scammell Routeman pushed the boundaries in glass reinforced plastic cab technology

Not all companies adopted glass reinforced plastic cabs for their vehicles and of those that did, many reverted back to steel-sides, especially when the likes of Motor Panels and the Willenhall Motor Radiator Company were providing complete cabs ready-made. Motor Panels cabs appeared on models by Argyle, ERF, Guy, and Thornycroft. The LAD (Leyland-Albion-Dodge) Vista Vue was a particularly striking design with very fluid lines that stepped in above the headlights and radiator grille, and again just below the windscreen. This type was used by Leyland on their Comet, Albion for the Reiver range, the Dodge 300 series and Scammell's Trunker.

For 1958, AEC revamped its Mammoth Major rigid six and eight-wheelers which were offered with a choice of cabs according to customer taste. These were fitted by AEC's subsidiary coachbuilding division, Park Royal Vehicles. Six years later, AEC had become part of the Leyland Group and the Mammoth Major was marketed

ABOVE 1965 Leyland Beaver Power Plus with the LAD Vista Vue cab

with Leyland's Ergomatic tilt cab.

Some vehicles, especially delivery vans were provided with sliding entrance doors that, when open, protruded little beyond the overall width of the vehicle. It also meant that getting in and out was easier in tight parking spaces compared to a vehicle fitted with conventional hinged doors.

At the beginning of the 1960s, BMC introduced the Austin/Morris FG range to replace a dated split-screen FE series. The cab design on the FG was regarded at the time as extraordinarily ground-breaking and had some very interesting idiosyncrasies.

On the front corners, below the windscreen, were two small kerbside-view windows which not only allowed the driver to place the vehicle close to the pavement but eliminated a blind spot. The most innovative feature was the entrance doors which were located at an angle on each of the rear corners of the cab. This in effect gave the same sort of benefit afforded by a sliding door as, again, when open, neither the nearside nor the offside door protruded more than a few inches from the overall cab width. In practice, the FG did come in for some criticism, however, as for some, the angled doors were too narrow and their positioning meant that the seats were also rather cramped especially with the engine taking up a lot of room between driver and passenger.

RIGHT This AEC Mercury articulated tractor unit dates from 1970 and features the Ergomatic cab that was also used on other trucks within the Leyland Group

In 1972, Dennis Brothers of Guildford who had stoically remained an independent concern were finally subject of a takeover bid when Hestair Group (formerly the Heston Aircraft Company of Hounslow) bought them out. Hestair already owned the assets of Yorkshire Vehicles, itself a descendant of the Yorkshire Patent Steam Wagon Company of Leeds. From then on Dennis's capacity as a truck manufacturer was in the production of export models only. The last major

development as far as the company was concerned was a cab designed by Tom Karen at David Ogle Ltd in Letchworth. This styling house had been responsible for such creations as the Bond Bug, Reliant Robin, Reliant Scimitar GTE, Raleigh Chopper and in 1976, Luke Skywalker's landspeeder for the film Star Wars Episode IV: A New Hope! Two years later Karen penned a very square box cab for the Perkins or Gardner-engine 16-ton Dennis Delta but it was not popular.

ABOVE The quite distinctive BMC FG cab used by Morris and Austin was not universally popular with drivers. Entrance doors were located on the rear corners of the cab and interior comfort was further compromised by the engine cover

The pictures in this book were provided courtesy of the following:

THE REFERENCE LIBRARY

THE MOTORING PICTURE LIBRARY
NATIONAL MOTOR MUSEUM, BEAULIEU

Research and input courtesy of:

MIKE LANHAM

Design & Artwork: ALEX YOUNG

Published by: DEMAND MEDIA LIMITED & G2 ENTERTAINMENT LIMITED

Publishers: JASON FENWICK & JULES GAMMOND

Written by: STEVE LANHAM